NEOCOLONIALISM IN WEST AFRICA

A Collection of Essays and Articles

REVISED EDITION

CHERNOH ALPHA M. BAH

Africanist
PRESS

Philadelphia

Neocolonialism in West Africa
A Collection of Essays & Articles
Revised Edition
First published in Bloomington, Indiana 2014 by iUniverse LLC.
Revised Edition 2016 by Africanist Press.

Africanist Press books may be ordered through booksellers or by contacting:
Africanist Press
5114 Race Street
Philadelphia, PA 19139
www.africanistpress.com

+1-347-569-1978 (United States)
Email: africanists@yahoo.com • africanistpress100@gmail.com

ISBN 978-0-9969739-3-9 (paperback)

Printed in the United States of America.

To my son, Allieu M. Bah; and my wife, Isatu Bah.

CONTENTS

A Foreword
to the Revised Edition

In early 2014, I was living in Edmonton, Canada. A year earlier, I had returned to the United States after a brief and disastrous volunteering stint with the United States Government in a small country in West Africa to which I had been randomly assigned. That country was Sierra Leone.

My early-terminated volunteering stint in Sierra Leone had deeply affected me personally and politically. I had gone into the country as a young American feigning idealism, eager to shore up a then-unnamed intuition, which had been haunting me; that something was fundamentally wrong with the way the world was organized. I'd recently graduated from a small, public university in Utah, where I'd spent two out of four years without a bed, often unable to afford groceries. My fellow volunteers, while personally kind and intelligent people, were predominately upper-middle class youths, recently graduated from private liberal-arts colleges. Maybe this difference in our life experiences contributed to our varied reactions to our deployment in Sierra Leone – I can't fully say. But I noticed that their response to encountering the abject poverty of one of the world's poorest countries was, first and foremost, personal. I, however, became political. My relative wealth of opportunity and privilege, as a citizen and representative of the most powerful country on Earth, became the defining characteristic of my visit to this neocolonial "periphery."

I'd returned to America as a troubled young man with two questions on my mind: why are some peoples and regions of the world so impoverished while others are so wealthy, and what can be done to change this fact? These questions led me down a path of critical, radicalizing literature. I began broaching taboo topics, reading the work of individuals such as Che Guevara, Noam Chomsky, and Frantz Fanon (at one point, a box of radical books in my truck earned me hours of detention and interrogation by the Canadian Border Services Agency).

I begin to notice a serious deficiency in radical literature, however, especially in regards to West Africa, and also in regards to concrete, contextualized analyses for our contemporary times. The literature seemed either to ignore global political economy and the significance of Africa for understanding contemporary global capitalism, or else it was written prior to the 1970s. The lack of meaningful struggle for political power has become endemic across the global left – which seems comfortable in limiting itself solely to cultural questions or theoretical philosophizing.

With this backdrop, it seemed absolutely serendipitous when one day I encountered a book, published that very same week in March 2014, entitled *Neocolonialism in West Africa*. I was even more surprised to learn that the author was a Sierra Leonean named Chernoh Alpha M. Bah, a serious political actor who also led a socialist movement within the country and the region.

Here was the book (and the movement) I'd been looking for, a book not only applicable to my own focus, but a book which brought the great theoretical and historical works of the revolutionary tradition down to Earth for the twenty-first century.

Chernoh Bah's *Neocolonialism in West Africa* is a revolutionary text, a call to action for the working classes of Africa and, specifically, the Mano-River Sub-region (Sierra Leone, Liberia, and Guinea-Conakry). In the same vein as classic, contextualized analyses and theoretical applications such as Lenin's *What is to Be Done* or the speeches of Amilcar Cabral, *Neocolonialism in West Africa* is a series of essays and articles written for specific purposes in the midst of an ongoing revolutionary struggle.

Because of the organic nature of the book's composition, it allows for an unfiltered, intimate glance into the inner-workings of a complex political situation, of a country, of a region, and of a people struggling against all odds for meaningful democracy and control of their own resources in the wake of a decade-long civil war. In this life or death struggle, the stakes could not be higher. The book offers an account of what the on-the-ground realities of neocolonialism look like today, especially during periods of neoliberal elections. The work brings concrete insights into the collusion between powerful multi-national interests and the capitalist state. In fact, the book can be taken as a one-of-a-kind case study of the mechanisms and dimensions of the state, of culture, of ethnicity and identity, and of capital within West Africa in the neoliberal era.

The book offers an especially useful insight into the workings of state and corporate media propaganda, while simultaneously illustrating how to confront this propaganda head-on, using the same mass media against itself. Bah is himself a journalist, after-all, and remains the most consistent and substantive voice of opposition within the Sierra Leone press.

Bah initially published this book through a print-on-demand service – an increasingly popular and useful outlet for independent writers hoping to publish their works and breach the iron-walled exclusivity of contemporary capitalist publishing. Unfortunately, the limitations and unethical practices of the print-on-demand and self-publishing industry became obvious to Bah and all others involved throughout the course of promoting this work. Bah undertook a world tour to push the book, an endeavor I joined him for shortly in New York City in June 2014, selling hundreds of copies. We watched as hundreds more sold online. Crucially, the funds from the book were to be used for the all-important endeavors of political organizing and party-registration in Sierra Leone – an expensive task given the limitations the Sierra Leone government has placed upon democracy by requiring large sums of money to register a party (fail to pay, and one risks arrest for engaging in unofficial political activity). So we were both confused and dismayed when we noticed that the amount of money coming in from online sales was not commensurate to the thousands of copies sold. To this day, the profit from hundreds of books remains unaccounted for by *iUniverse*, a division of *Author Solutions LLC*, an Indiana-based publishing company.

That's one reason this book is due for a new edition. The correction of a number of grammatical errors is another. But, more importantly, in the nearly three years which have passed since the book was originally compiled, Bah's analysis and critique of Sierra Leone's authoritarian neocolonial state and the predictions he made concerning its trajectory have been proven presciently accurate, as the conduct of state officials, international research institutions and corporations, and of the imperialist powers during the 2014 Ebola outbreak clearly illustrate.

From Chernoh Bah's prediction that the Koroma administration would attempt to hold on to power beyond its constitutional-limit of two terms, to his illustration of multinational and imperial exploitation of African resources at the expense of African lives, the book illuminates the last three years in new ways, providing much needed context and background, while continuing to provide useful analysis for where the country continues to head and how the people may best struggle in their efforts to reform the nation and the region, especially as elections draw near once again.

In the years since the book was released, *Africanist Press*, a longtime outlet for the publishing of the ASM newspaper, *The Africanist Bulletin*, and also a platform for publishing updates on the Ebola Outbreak to protect and inform citizens of the region throughout 2014 and 2015, has been expanded under the cooperation of Bah and other writers and activists to include book publishing. In late 2015, Africanist Press published its first book title, also written by Bah, *The Ebola Outbreak in West Africa: Corporate Gangsters, Multinationals, and Rogue Politicians*. In many ways, these two books can be seen as companions – *Neocolonialism in West Africa* offers the economic and political analysis that comprises the setting for the investigative journalistic research of *The Ebola Outbreak in West Africa*.

It is the publisher's hope that this new edition will continue to inspire and inform the radical struggle for democratic rights and human dignity now taking place in West Africa, while also informing progressive minded individuals of the dynamics of contemporary revolutionary struggle in Africa. And it is my hope that individuals like Chernoh Bah and works like *Neocolonialism in West Africa* continue to surface in these tumultuous times, as a response to the ravages of capitalism and imperialism upon the most vulnerable populations of the Earth.

Joshua Lew McDermott
President
ASM International Support Committee
Pittsburg, USA

FOREWORD

I first met Chernoh Alpha M. Bah in 2005 in London while working with an organization committed to the revolutionary transformation of African people all over the world. My task was to search for individuals and organizations willing to attend a conference in London that would build a global revolutionary organization to lead the struggle for socialism and continental unity in Africa.

Chernoh Alpha M. Bah, the leader of the Africanist Movement (now African Socialist Movement) of West Africa, responded to my invitation enthusiastically. He traveled to London where I helped to host him while he formally met members of the organization. He later traveled to the United States on a speaking tour few months after the London trip to win international support for his organization and the struggle for socialism in Sierra Leone. During one of Chernoh Alpha M. Bah's speaking tours in the United States, he and I also spent time together. I later traveled to Sierra Leone as a guest of Chernoh Bah and the Africanist Movement where I also participated in meetings in Guinea and Sierra Leone. Since then, we have remained close as Chernoh Bah continues his political work in Sierra Leone and other parts of the world.

It did not take long to discover Chernoh Alpha M. Bah's fervent commitment to the freedom of African people. His singular focus is apparent in all he does. As a journalist, he gives cutting-edge analysis of the crisis of neocolonialism in West Africa and beyond; as an organizer, he has constructed and commanded a force of dispossessed youth dissatisfied with the conditions forced upon them by neo-colonialist politicians. It would seem there is no place that is too far; there is no work that is too hard; and there is no struggle too intimidating in Chernoh Alpha M. Bah's quest for the people's liberation.

In this era of neocolonialism, African people need champions, such as Chernoh Alpha M. Bah. More than half a century of independence from colonizing nations has yielded no progress for the masses of African people. Kwame Nkrumah, Frantz Fanon, Walter Rodney, and others warned our people that "flag independence" would mean nothing if the economic relationship between the colonizer and colonized remained the same. And these great African patriots have been proven right. Under this new form of colonialism, Africa continues to be sucked dry of its natural resources while millions of its people are saddled with an oppressive and impoverished existence. Sierra Leone, which is Chernoh Bah's place of birth, is a fitting example of this situation.

Sierra Leone has been placed at the bottom of the global ladder of development. Most development indices classify the country among the world's poorest countries despite its vast natural resources. When I visited Sierra Leone some years ago as a guest of Chernoh Bah, I saw the under-development with my own eyes: there was no electricity, no water supply, no proper infrastructure, no good roads, no proper healthcare, and no sign of good governance. I saw the missing limbs of men, women, and children who were victims of the bloody conflict for Sierra Leone's diamond wealth. But I also saw a champion—a man who will not rest until Africa once again knows freedom and enjoys the proceeds of its natural wealth.

This is the information contained in *Neocolonialism in West Africa: A Collection of Essays and Articles* by Chernoh Alpha M. Bah. The publication of this collection of essays is timely, for African people must be armed with the ideology of freedom. From the early days of slavery and colonialism, there have been those Africans trained by missionaries, schooled in the universities of the west, indoctrinated by the ideas of western philosophers, and inculcated the values of western culture displayed through the media. Rarely are we exposed to the philosophy of Kwame Nkrumah, Marcus Garvey, Walter Rodney, Sekou Toure, Thomas Sankara, and other African heroes. The ideas that are forced upon us help us to accept our place of subservience in the world. These ideas teach us that Africa needs foreign investors to continue to plunder its resources rather than African businesses that can develop these resources. These ideas teach us that the African way of life is inferior and the European way of life is superior, and we should adopt this European lifestyle.

In the face of this ideological assault, Chernoh Bah's collection of essays takes on critical significance. He provides a very clear picture, filled with specific details, of the failure of neo-colonialism. Chernoh Bah's *Neocolonialism in West Africa: A Collection of Essays and Articles* provide the unfiltered truth about the plight of the people of West Africa. And anyone seeking a better understanding of how imperialism functions in West Africa must have this book.

Chernoh Alpha M. Bah embodies the legacy of I.T.A Wallace-Johnson and other African freedom fighters. Wallace-Johnson was a journalist, activist, organizer, and politician—roles that Chernoh Bah plays today. Just as Wallace Johnson was a thorn on the side of the British colonial authorities, so is Chernoh Bah a force to be reckoned with in the neocolonial era. In the history of Africa, many stepped forward in the battle against colonialism, but the battle is far from over. The demise of neocolonialism will never be realized without the unity of the African masses, organized with a new breed of leadership that will usher in a new era of African prosperity free from the shackles of the past. Chernoh Alpha M. Bah has stood up and has been counted, and he challenges the masses to do the same.

Natalio Sowande Wheatley, PhD
Lecturer
H. Lavity Stoutt Community College
The British Virgin Islands

PREFACE

A journalist that works for a leading newspaper in Sierra Leone once asked me why I have consistently refused to join the ruling class elite in Sierra Leone. He asked: why are you appearing unnecessarily stubborn when you can easily find your way into the ruling class and forget every other issue?

This is a question that I have been confronted with since I was a child and more so after I had resolved to engage myself in political work to resolve the contradictions facing my people.

The endemic poverty and suffering that have surrounded my life in Sierra Leone have always made me inquisitive. I have always wondered at the sight and plight of suffering mothers and their children in my neighborhood. The daily struggles of market women and peasant mothers struggling just to cook a single meal a day for their families, the presence of the many unemployed youth on the streets, and the roaming jobless fathers hanging around my neighborhood created images of despair and desolation in my mind, even as a boy. These were images of a hopeless population who were uncertain about their future. Their arguments and dreams of a better future, the endless discussions they had with one another that attempted to explain the causes of the many social and economic challenges faced by the majority of families across the country, constantly haunted my thinking as a child.

I have never stopped thinking about these images of frustration that accompanied the obvious disillusionment of my community. These were images that pricked my sense of imagination as a child. They were the images of despair and dissolution paradoxically produced by an empty determination of a dispossessed population. These never-ending frustrations and despair formed, and continue to form, the agenda of the informal congregations in my community. As a child, I sought answers from young men and women who were older than me as to why things were this way. It was obvious that anger was rife not just in my neighborhood but also in all communities across the country.

This was in the mid-1980s when a corrupt government controlled by a bankrupt and inept political leadership ruined the country and undermined the potential for economic and social development. Public infrastructure including roads, hospitals, electricity supply, educational standards and public transportation facilities had all collapsed during this period. The country was in a serious crisis of development. School teachers had gone several months without pay, College campuses were routinely closed due to frequent strikes, doctors and nurses faced the worse conditions of employment, commodity prices were constantly sky-rocketing, opposition political parties had been banned from operation, police brutality and state sponsored murders were rampant across the country. Poverty rates became exponentially alarming; a state of political terror and violence characterized the political atmosphere of the country. This was the era of a one party dictatorship that started in 1978 under the leadership of the All Peoples Congress (APC) government of President Siaka Stevens.

The growing statistic of poverty fuelled by declining standards of living produced by poor economic policies of a repressive regime had created mass discontent among citizens in the 1980s. A discourse anchored on the need for a revolutionary transformation of the country formed the agenda of all formal and informal gatherings of young people across the country at the time. Reports that a potential armed struggle against the government was about to begin were rumored during private discussions of many households. These rumors were discussed in fear by families whose spirits had been beaten into submission by the repressive tendencies of an obviously failed regime.

Siaka Stevens was Sierra Leone's first president. He was a direct benefactor of the British strategy to de-radicalize the militant tendency of the trade union movement in Sierra Leone.

Siaka Stevens came to power in 1968, a year after the controversial elections of 1967. In that election held on March 17, 1967, Siaka Stevens and his All Peoples Congress (APC) reportedly won a narrow margin against the incumbent Prime Minister, Albert Margai of the Sierra Leone Peoples Party (SLPP). Stevens was overthrown in an army coup few minutes after he was declared to have won the elections. He was returned to power a year later, after a brief period of military rule.

In April 1971, Siaka Stevens commenced a program of personalizing governance. He enacted a new Constitution that gave him more executive powers. Seven years later, in 1978, he transformed the country into a one-party state. He banned all opposition to his government and out-lawed the existence of rival political parties in the country. The All Peoples Congress (APC) was the only party that was allowed to operate in Sierra Leone.

I was born a year after the introduction of Siaka Stevens' one-party dictatorship, on March 28, 1979 in Mandurie, a small village West of Bombali district in the north of the country. By 1989, ten years after I was born, the political atmosphere in West Africa had drastically changed. In neighboring Liberia, the National Patriotic Front of Liberia (NPFL), a rebel movement led by Charles Taylor, faced the regime of Samuel Doe, a military officer who came to power in a bloody coup in 1980, with a rebellion. The NPFL rebellion, believed to have been sponsored by the United States government, had made popular headlines on the western media. Photographs of Charles Taylor and his gun-toting rebel soldiers – mostly in their early 20s - recruited from Liberia's alienated youths, fascinated our imagination.

Taylor, who was an employee of the Doe government, crossed into Liberia from Ivory Coast on Christmas Eve of 1989 to wage a guerrilla war against his former ally. Taylor was reported to have broken out of prison in the United States where he was awaiting extradition to Liberia on charges of corruption. By mid-1990, most of the country was controlled by Taylor's rebel fighters.

In Sierra Leone, people watched the progressive demise of Samuel Doe's government. On September 9, 1990 news broke-out that Doe has been captured by rebel fighters led by Prince Johnson. Few days later, video images of the torture and execution of Samuel Doe was released to the world. This video footage showed Doe's naked body as he was being tortured, his ears being cut off along with some of his fingers and toes. The spectacle of this torture was the subject of discussion in Sierra Leone, where rumors of a pending rebel attack was also wide spread.

I was eleven years old when this was happening. As kids we enacted the torture of Samuel Doe and his executions. Few months later, on March 23, 1991, the Revolutionary United Front (RUF) attacked Sierra Leone. The British Broadcasting Corporation (BBC) in London aired an interview with Foday Sankoh, who claimed to be leading the rebellion against the APC misrule of the country. Sankoh was a former corporal in the Sierra Leone Army and had been dismissed following alleged involvement in a military coup against the APC in the 1970s.

News of the RUF attack was not taken seriously in Sierra Leone. The Sierra Leone army was ill equipped and unprepared for the war. Siaka Stevens had transferred power to Joseph Saidu Momoh by this time. President Momoh and his colleagues looted state resources to the point that the state was unable to supply basic services. Poverty in the rural areas was rife and rural peoples were completely isolated from Freetown. The excessive corruption of the regime had made it completely unpopular amongst the country's citizens.

As a youth, I had joined some of the student and youth organizations in my school and township, and we discussed the advancing war. Every day, stories of the progress of the rebellion and the effort of the army to repel the rebel advance into the eastern part of the country constituted the discussions among young people. The government immediately announced a national program of army recruitments. They wanted to increase the numbers of the national army in response to the rebellion. A year later, on April 29, 1992 a few junior officers of the Sierra Leone Army who had gone to Freetown from the war-front announced that they had overthrown the APC regime from power. The APC had been removed from power by the National Provisional Ruling Council (NPRC), led by Captain Valentine Strasser, a 27-year-old officer. The overthrow of the APC one-party dictatorship was enthusiastically received by the mass of the country.

However, the APC's removal from power did not end the armed conflict. Foday Sankoh's armed rebellion intensified. The military regime itself relapsed into corruption and mismanagement of public resources. In the countryside, the war escalated and spread into the north of the country. Whole communities were destroyed and hundreds of people were rendered homeless. Atrocities of the RUF became horrifying and alarming. In Freetown, the military government became largely unpopular because of corruption. During this period, mass recruitment into the national army had also polarized the military.

By 1995, a national campaign for the return to civil rule was mounted in the country. Pro-democracy organizations and civil society groups organized to demand elections and the end of military rule. The army appeared unwilling to relinquish power. They finally did after the elections of 1996. Much of the political history of the 1990s was punctuated by armed violence, military coups and war. By 2000, the country had the largest number of foreign troops in the world as part of United Nations military intervention. This was after the death toll had been risen to alarming heights. Images of innocent women and children, who had lost limbs in the war, were broadcast by the western media into the living rooms of families in Europe and North America. The atrocities of the conflict in Sierra Leone were now considered unprecedented in recent history by western governments. Thousands had already died and many homes had been destroyed before the western media engaged the conflict. This devastating war was declared ended in 2002.

On November 17, 2012 the people of Sierra Leone went to the polls to elect a new president and a total of one hundred and twelve members of parliament. The elections were the third since the end of the country's ten-year old civil conflict. The previous elections were in 2007 and were reportedly won by the All Peoples Congress (APC) under the leadership of Ernest Bai Koroma, the current president, who beat out the Sierra Leone Peoples Party (SLPP). The APC and the SLPP have been the only ruling political groups in the country for the last fifty years.

Sierra Leone's development and growth have been ruined by the political elite of these two parties, who inherited a subservient economy and political system bequeathed by British colonizers in the 1960s. They have kept the masses in a horrible state of perpetual poverty and hopelessness. Constituting less than two percent of the country's population, this group of middle class politicians – protected by Britain and its western allies – has sold out the future of the country to a consortium of multinational corporations.

Today, multinational corporations that include African Minerals, London Mining, African Petroleum, Addax Bioenergy Group, Socfin International and a host of others exploit the vast mineral and energy resources of the country.

Large-scale agricultural corporations from Europe have recently taken over thousands of farmlands from rural communities. A new shift in the pattern of "corporate colonialism" is now in motion with issues of land grabbing by western agricultural companies. Renewed conflicts and protests over the nature of the agreements between the government and these new agricultural corporations typify the recent crisis of capitalist development in the region. International financial institutions and western capitalist corporations who promote economic programs that undermine the welfare of the masses dominate the economy of Sierra Leone.

During the last fifty years, Sierra Leone has been continuously rated as "one of the worst places to be in the world." The United Nations consistently reported that the country is the "least developed" in the world with the highest infant and maternal mortality rates, a life expectancy that is below forty years and an economy that is heavily looted by multinational corporate agencies and international financial institutions.

Regardless of the fact that the country is home to the world's finest diamonds, Sierra Leone still retains the unenviable reputation of owning the most horrible statistics on health, education, poor human development and the near absence of infrastructural development.

For over fifty years since Sierra Leone's so-called independence, only the middle class elites of the APC and SLPP have controlled and governed the country. They have proficiently developed a vicious system that facilitates their permanent recycling from one position of power to another. Politics and power have served as the basis for their own upliftment as a class. They have collectively utilized the immense resources of the country to change their own material conditions and standard of life, yet have provided almost nothing but misery and poverty for the ordinary masses. The conditions of the workers and peasants remain insufferable and grow worse on a daily basis.

In the last elections, a group of African men and women determined to challenge the political monopoly of the APC and SLPP participated in the elections. I led this group of men and women, organized under the umbrella of the African Socialist Movement (ASM).

After having witnessed much of the history of oppressive politics and economic exploitation of the country for the last thirty-five years of my life, I resolved to build the African Socialist Movement (ASM) in November 2009 following the dissolution of the Africanist Movement in October of the same year.

The Africanist Movement was formed as a revolutionary mass movement to fight for the liberation and unification of Africa and African people under an all-African socialist state. Having lived and worked as a journalist and political activist, I had come to the conclusion that the political instability in West Africa as epitomized by the history of unprogressive politics prevalent in Sierra Leone could only be reversed through an effort to overturn the social structure upon which such a system is built. This is what triggered me to organize the many unemployed and exploited young people in Sierra Leone into building an organization that is committed to challenging the existing political groups whose rivalry for power has plunged our communities into endless crisis and poverty.

Key to my understanding is the fact that the struggle against the imperialist and neocolonialist forces in Sierra Leone falls within the global struggle for African unity and socialism.

To accomplish this monumental task, the African Socialist Movement (ASM) arguably constitutes the most advanced element of the working class and peasant movement in Sierra Leone. In the last elections of 2012, the ASM evolved a strategic relationship and alliance with a pro-democratic party, the National Democratic Alliance (NDA), in Sierra Leone. The principal motive for such an arrangement was anchored in the need to build and advance a national movement with a strategy guided by revolutionary leaders in a bid to enhance a national democratic transition involving all workers and peasants. In the view and conclusion of the ASM, the middle class politicians in Sierra Leone, divided along the APC and SLPP, cannot be defeated without a popular movement involving the general mass of the country.

This was the objective that led to the political coalition between the ASM and the National Democratic Alliance (NDA). This political coalition was of necessity in Sierra Leone in that period because the organizational capacity and strength of the workers and peasants is still in an embryonic stage. In a political environment where five decades of social oppression and economic exploitation have heightened the indices of poverty and hopelessness, the ability to sustain a mass struggle is extremely difficult. As part of the strategic objective to wage a struggle against the neocolonialist and imperialist forces currently in power in Sierra Leone, I have resigned myself to engage, alongside the ASM, in a struggle to change the horrible situation in the country; a situation that has resulted from more than five decades of unchallenged APC and SLPP monopoly of power.

This book, therefore, constitutes a documentary of my thoughts and efforts to resolve and challenge the organized political dictatorship, social oppression and economic exploitation that continue to exist in Sierra Leone, and all of West Africa. The country is still governed by politically bankrupt elite who sees power as the license to selfishly accumulate wealth at the expense of the real development of the people. Such a system of social and political injustice must be challenged. This is the information that this collection of essays and articles sought to convey. It is an appeal to the conscience of freedom loving people around the world to stand-up against global injustice and international exploitation.

Chernoh Alpha M. Bah
Freetown

INTRODUCTION

> *"The neo-colonialism of today represents imperialism in its final and perhaps its most dangerous stage. Old-fashioned colonialism is by no means entirely abolished. It still constitutes an African problem. In place of colonialism as the main instrument of imperialism we have today neo-colonialism. The essence of neo-colonialism is that the State, which is subject to it, is, in theory, independent and has all the outward trappings of international sovereignty. In reality its economic system and thus its political policy is directed from outside. The methods and form of this direction can take various shapes. For example, in an extreme case the troops of the imperial power may garrison the territory of the neo-colonial State and control the government of it. More often, however, neo-colonialist control is exercised through economic or monetary means. The neo-colonial State may be obliged to take the manufactured products of the imperialist power to the exclusion of competing products from elsewhere..."*
>
> Kwame Nkrumah[1]

The withdrawal of European colonialist officials from Africa by the middle of the twentieth century was not the end of colonialism on the continent. Neither was the departure a result of willful efforts on the part of the various European governments to genuinely leave the continent. This retreat was largely due to the changing dynamics of the international political scene following the end of the European wars of 1939-1945. The end of the second imperialist war created the genesis of a severe crisis for western colonialism; a situation generated by the rising resistance of oppressed and colonized peoples around the world against capitalist colonialism spearheaded by Western Europe.

In Africa, there were major events in the anti-colonialist struggle on the

---

[1] Kwame Nkrumah (1966). *Neocolonialism, The Last Stage of Imperialism*. International Publishers: London. Kwame Nkrumah was the leader of the Convention Peoples Party (CPP) and was Ghana's first president. He was also the first anti-colonial leader to win independence in West Africa.

continent. A few of the most notable are the armed struggle of the Kenya Land and Freedom Army known as the Mau Mau against British colonialism, the positive action campaign of the Convention Peoples Party (CPP) of Kwame Nkrumah in Ghana, the defiance of France by the Parti Democratique de la Guinee (PDG) of Ahmed Sekou Toure in Guinea, and the armed struggle against Portuguese colonialism by the African Party for the Independence of Guinea and Cape Verde (PAIGC) headed by Amilcar Cabral. It was the intensity of these campaigns, especially the guerilla struggles of African freedom fighters in Zimbabwe and Mozambique, which threatened and undermined the ability of Europeans to continue their policy of direct political and economic control over the territories of the continent.

In West Africa, the independence of Ghana in 1957 and the dramatic withdrawal of Guinea from Charles De Gaulle's proposal of a French Community in 1958 marked the climax of the "decolonization process" in the region. By 1961, nearly all of West Africa was completely under the control of African political elites with new territories, national anthems and flags. While this era was characterized by the start of a new period, developments on the continent generated several questions that have remained either persistently unanswered or satisfactorily unresolved.

The so-called post-colonial realities in Africa seem to be challenging the ability of African people to independently run their own affairs. It appears that the years of so-called independence meant absolutely nothing. The conditions in Africa remain dismal and the living circumstances of African people have changed for the worse after the transition to so-called independence. There is an argument that Africa was better under direct colonialism than it is today. Those who advance such an argument are not forced to assume such a position due to whatever development colonialism bequeathed to the post-colonial leadership of the continent. As Walter Rodney aptly stated, "For the first three decades of colonialism, hardly anything was done that could remotely be termed a service to the African people. It was in fact only after the last war that social services were built as a matter of policy."[2] So the modern-day criticism of the post-colonial leadership is not necessarily the result of an effort to justify the colonial era. The statistics, which show that today, Africa is underdeveloped, are the statistics representing the state of affairs at the end of colonialism. For that matter, the figures at the end of the first decade of African independence in spheres such as health, housing and education are often several times higher than the figures inherited by the newly independent governments (Rodney 1972). The current criticism of African political leaders is the consequence of disillusionment at the quality of leadership and governance culture provided by the African political elite who inherited the state machinery

---

[2] Walter Rodney (1972). . Bogle L'Ouverture Publications: London

of the colonizers.

The continent is still plagued with severe problems of social and economic development. This is coupled with massive population unemployment and under-employment. Poverty rates have remained alarming. Ironically, the political elites have grown extremely wealthy and brutally repressive in all corners of the continent despite the continuation of mass poverty. The same questions generated by the contradictions of colonial times have persisted. With over fifty years of so-called independence, why does Africa still face some of the most devastating challenges and problems in the world? What is responsible for the numerous socio-economic and political contradictions that continue to threaten peace, growth and development on the continent? And why has continental unity become an illusion and seemingly impossible task?

The answers to these questions form part of the mainstream discourse on the obstacles presented by the "post-colonial realties" on the continent today. The discourses have not only attempted to solve the historical circumstances of the "decolonization process" and its ultimate results, but they have equally set in motion the processes for the rigorous understanding, or even investigation, of the modus operandi of the so-called post-colonial state. An analysis of the operational methods of the African state as bequeathed to the African political elite will help provide a better understanding of the current situational challenges confronting Africa today. An analysis will also help answer specifically the questions regarding citizenship, underdevelopment, famine, resource exploitation and international affairs; all of which have served as catalysts for political instability, civil conflict and economic crisis.

It is through such a social post-mortem that we will fully grasp the true form and nature of the political economy of the post-colonial arrangement and its relationship with erstwhile colonial administrations on the continent. This investigation will squarely have as its principal objective the discovery of the nature of independence won by Africans: Was the transition from direct white rule to black government or self-government a transition to actual independence, or was the change of leadership a transition to a new form of colonization?

In his book, *Neocolonialism, The Last Stage of Imperialism*[3], Kwame Nkrumah stated clearly that this transition did not result in independence but in a new form of colonialism aptly described as neocolonialism.

The rising resistance of colonized peoples across the world forced the colonial powers to change their methods and tactics of political control. They dispensed their flags and their most hated European officials on the continent, the expatriate staff. In turn, they imposed on the people African politicians who were still subject to the dictates and control of the former colonial powers.

---

[3] Nkrumah, 1966

As Nkrumah said, "this means that they were "giving independence" to former subjects, to be followed by 'aid' for their development," but in actual fact, the European powers had already devised innumerable ways to accomplish objectives formerly achieved by naked colonialism. It is the sum total of these modern attempts to perpetuate colonialism while at the same time talking about 'freedom', which has come to be known as neocolonialism.

According to Kwame Nkrumah, neocolonialism is the worst form of imperialism. For a country under neocolonial control, it means political power without responsibility. The citizens of a neocolonial state suffer from external economic exploitation without redress. The differences between colonialism and neocolonialism lie in the principal fact that, under colonialism, the imperialist power was at least obliged to justify to its own citizens, the actions it was taking in the colonial territory. And in the colonial territory itself, those who served the ruling imperial power could at least look to its protection against any violent move by their opponents. With neocolonialism, all this became practically impossible.

Under neocolonialism, the hand of the colonizing nation is ably disguised. It is always hidden behind the backs of the indigenous politicians educated and propped to power by the colonizing nation. The politicians of the colonizing state provide military and technical support to the politicians of the neocolonial state, in exchange for the natural resources and wealth of the colonial territory. The life and legitimacy of a neocolonial regime and the political stability of the country itself, depends on how much access, control and benefit is exercised and derived from it by the colonizing nation. Where the strategic economic interests of the colonizing nation appears to be threatened or undermined by the policy directives or actions of the neocolonialist politicians, the political legitimacy of the government of such a territory faces the risk of an opposition, from both internal and external forces, aligned to the interests and goals of the imperialist nation.

The main objective of the neocolonial project is the creation of a state, which is theoretically independent with all the trappings of international sovereignty, but whose economic system and political development is directed from the outside.

This book is an attempt to expose the problems that have accompanied the transition from "direct European rule" to so-called "African self-government". It presents an argument that the transition was not a change in the colonial bureaucratic structure but a continuation of the exploitative arrangement of the European colonialist state. Today, while indigenous politicians seemingly dominate the African political scene, the political economy is directly controlled by European powers. The ongoing crisis and conflict, and attendant negative consequences have been the result of the continuing scramble for the immense resources on the continent.

Although the emphasis of the narratives in this book is centered on the countries of the Mano River area (Guinea, Sierra Leone, and Liberia), the episodes addressed herein are shared by Africa on a continental level. The choice of the area covered in the book is motivated by three principal objectives. First, the Mano River countries are within one of the most resource-rich regions of the continent and are therefore an area of real or potential interest to western imperialist nations. Second, the area has also witnessed a greater level of instability and has also recorded a greater proportion of military coups, civil conflicts and national rebellions. Many of these unstable political developments are perfect examples of the general crisis and challenges of the "post-colonial" situation in Africa. These events are treated in this book as direct results of the neocolonial project and tied directly to the global contest for resource control by western powers. Most importantly, the countries of the Mano River area – Sierra Leone, Liberia and Guinea – share a strong history of cultural affinity. The ethnographical and demographical dynamics of the area are strikingly similar, which clearly inform the pattern and nature of the conflicts and crisis that have engulfed the area in recent decades.

This book comprises of selected essays and articles covering specific episodes and questions on recent political developments mainly in Sierra Leone and Guinea Conakry. These articles and essays are mainly written from the ideological perspective of the African Socialist Movement. These are largely articles and essays published over the last ten years detailing my opinion on significant developments within countries already mentioned. Some of these essays and articles have been re-edited and re-arranged to fit into the requirements of this book.

The book is therefore not principally the result of a conventional academic process, but an effort to explain the "post-colonial" conflicts within the ramifications of the neocolonialist state. It is therefore a theoretical endeavor that is largely informed by a culture of resistance and ideology of liberation anchored on socialist conclusions. This theoretical exercise is motivated by West Africa's strong history of anti-colonial resistance and political activism. It is a documentary of evidence detailing the practical failures of the neocolonialist project in Africa. It is also an effort to theorize an organized response that seeks to challenge and overturn the political arrangement of the neocolonial bureaucratic structure. Thus this book is not only aimed at exposing the practical contradictions produced by the neocolonial project, but provides a clear thoughtful analysis of the modern forms and agencies of colonialist control in Africa and its consequences.

The significance of this book is that it seeks to rectify the limitations inherent in what Amilcar Cabral defined as "the struggle against our own weaknesses".[4] An effort to understanding the contradictions of a society should encompass a comprehensive investigation of both the external and internal contradictions of the given society. Such an investigation must consider, for its own validity,

---

[4] Amilcar Cabral, "*The Weapon of Theory*". Address delivered to the first Tricontinental Conference of the Peoples of Asia, Africa and Latin America held in Havana in January 1966.

an examination of all the economic, social, cultural and historical reality of the area in which such an effort is directed. An exercise of whatever nature, whether theoretical or otherwise, that is not based on knowledge of this fundamental reality, runs the grave risk of being condemned to failure (Cabral 1966).

This aforementioned understanding is the main thrust of this book. Its content addresses, not only an ideological question, but rectifies a theoretical vacuum that is required in the face of the ongoing conflicts and crisis produced by western economic interests. It situates the ongoing conflicts and instability in the region within the global contest for control of Africa's resources by western powers.

The content is divided into three main parts. Part one deals with the manifestations of neocolonialism. Using key ideological and theoretical methods to analyze key political events and questions, it gives a practical explanation of the workings of the neocolonial state actors. Part two addresses key questions relating to the internal conflicts of the African liberation movement. An analysis of the struggle between the African Socialist Movement (ASM) of Sierra Leone and the Uhuru Movement in Florida is presented in this section as an example. It deals with questions that hinder the movement against neocolonial rule on the continent. Part three, which would be considered as the main part of the book, deals squarely with the agencies and tools of neocolonialism. Through multinational corporations and elections, imperialist countries work to influence the outcome of political contests in West Africa in favor of parties and individuals supportive of the neocolonial agenda. This part of the book looks at the activities of multinational corporations in Guinea Conakry under General Lansana Conte and Sierra Leone from Ahmed Tejan Kabbah to Ernest Bai Koroma. The last chapter in particular deals squarely with contemporary issues around the style of governance of President Ernest Bai Koroma of Sierra Leone. It particularly warns that President Koroma is heading towards a path that nurtures an authoritarian democracy in Sierra Leone.

This collection of essays and articles are therefore expected to present not only a vivid understanding of the extant socio-political and economic contradictions facing the people of West Africa, but they will especially help African freedom fighters take note of the concrete observations that must be considered if the struggle against neocolonialism in Africa were to reach a desired objective: that of the liberation and unification of the continent under a socialist model of development.

PART ONE
MANIFESTATIONS OF NEOCOLONIALISM: SOME THEORETICAL & IDEOLOGICAL QUESTIONS

CHAPTER 1

THE ESSENCE OF POLITICAL IDEOLOGY: ADDRESSING THE THIRD FORCE ARGUMENT

Sierra Leone is one of the richest countries in the world in terms of natural resources. But statistics from agencies of the United Nations have always ranked its people as among the poorest in the world. These statistics of poverty and unemployment have been blamed on a corrupt political leadership and intensive multinational corporate activities in the country. For more than fifty years, only middle class politicians of the Sierra Leone Peoples Party (SLPP) and All Peoples Congress (APC) have governed the country. These groups of politicians have grown extremely wealthy by diverting revenue and resources from mining concessions into their private accounts while the rest of the population struggles without basic social services. For more than fifty years, efforts towards challenging the political monopoly of the SLPP and APC have only succeeded in strengthening their influence on the political landscape of the country. The country itself, split along ethno-regional lines by these two groups, continues to suffer from political corruption, poverty, massive youth unemployment, a declining economy and a crippling infrastructure. Political discourses on the way forward have been influenced by the existing ethno-regional dimensions. One school of thought believes that a solution to the problem is the creation of a "third party" that will bridge the ethnic and regional divide created by the SLPP and APC, which many blame for the underdevelopment of the country. In this article, Chernoh Alpha M. Bah examines the origin and limitations of the so-called "third force tendency" and argues that a solution to the problems created by the existing status quo is the overhaul of the entire social system. The article historically traces the origin of the ethno-regional divide to the colonial policy of the British, pointing out that it forms the basis for the creation of the neocolonial project in Sierra Leone. The article concludes that an ideology of liberation with self-determination as its objective will be the guiding worldview to defeat the social contradictions created *by the politicians of the APC and SLPP in Sierra Leone. This article was first published by the **Africanist Bulletin** in 2006 and later republished by **Africa News**.*

The reactionary effort of the African middle class politicians in Sierra Leone to defend their class interest has created vague ideas and arguments purposefully designed to distort efforts to organize for genuine liberation and unification of the oppressed masses against neocolonialist and imperialist oppression and exploitation.

This is not strange; however, as the African liberation movement in general is usually confronted with these obscuring ideas often emanating from the increasingly selfish ambitions of the African petty bourgeoisie to accomplish their immediate political and economic motives through the exploitation of the people's miserable conditions and aspirations for genuine change.

It is a major part of the battle of ideas. It is an ideological battle that constitutes a significant part of the struggle for self-determination and the continuous efforts of the masses to free themselves from the numerous contradictions facing them as a people. It becomes extremely significant in the struggle since it creates an opportunity to openly discuss and create a clear understanding of what the responsibility of the revolutionary organization should be to the people. Its appropriateness becomes obvious when it is seen as part of the desperate efforts to free the majority of exploited masses from the death-threatening conditions that they continuously face today because of the actions and inactions of a failed neocolonial system imposed on them by imperialism and its corporate allies.

This situation can only be understood and taken seriously by the mass of exploited people if it is addressed from the basis of a fundamental responsibility of the revolutionaries to put into clear and correct context certain debates around certain issues relating to social problems and the search for a concrete solution to resolve or put an end to such problems.

It is obvious today that in Sierra Leone, like any place in Africa, the country is faced with so many suggestions and opinions in the search for solutions. And the most difficult thing we are confronted with as well is the fact that even when these suggestions appear to identify the sources or circumstances of these problems, the suggestions themselves lack any ideological basis or explanation of the problems. In consequence, the suggestions themselves appear to revolve around the same contradictions. This has been and is still the most crucial issue we have to deal with in the struggle for self-determination especially so when certain sections of the people are now talking about a so-called "third force" approach to changing the current status quo.

Third force ideology is a reactionary argument

The argument advanced by "third force" proponents has its origin on the reactionary position that since the attainment of "independence," the country and its people are being controlled and governed by a single class of individuals who have proficiently developed a permanent system that facilitates their continuous recycling from one position of power to another. This system itself has consequently created a situation whereby possibility for access to power is only possible through a marriage or political baptism with the system. It is a system that has created the illusion that it is impossible for any neutral force not tied to its organizational arrangement to rise to power.

This year, the Sierra Leone Peoples Party (SLPP) had just celebrated ten years of its continuous stay in power with Ahmed Tejan Kabbah as president. Since 1996, the SLPP and Kabbah have been struggling and are still struggling to maintain control of political power regardless of ceaseless attempts that were made by both the army and the rebels of the Revolutionary United Front (RUF) to remove them from power. Kabbah himself is completing his second term as president of the country after he reportedly won two consecutive elections between 1996 and 2002.

The SLPP came to power as a consequence of the general campaign for democracy undertaken by the mass of ordinary people in 1995. At that time, the argument for a "ballot-box solution" to military rule – a legacy of the one party era – was so popular that it gave rise to the emergence of what was then called the "election before peace" movement. The belief was that only elections could end the people's problems.

Middle-class opportunism betrays the people and obscures the struggle

Consequently, the mass of the oppressed and poor people across the country was eventually miscarried to fight or struggle for a "ballot-box democracy," and they successfully removed a heinous military dictatorship from power. Unfortunately, they paved the way for the imposition of a neocolonial administration that represents the interests of Britain and its imperialist allies.

Today, the very people who formed the vanguard of that campaign are equally tongue-tied and completely bewildered. They can no longer understand how this cohort of middle class politicians manipulated their conditions in pursuit of their own selfish political aspirations.

The aspirations of the political class manifest themselves regularly, and they, ultimately, obscure the vision of the people for the future. So, it is important for the revolutionary organization to understand that it is the misleading actions and activities of this class of selfish kleptomaniacs that distort the efforts and aspirations of the masses to genuinely free themselves from the numerous contradictions they are faced with as a people. And the reality is that the status quo is formed primarily to serve the interest of this class, and its continuous existence depends on the oppression and denial of the people's right to be a self-determining people.

In Sierra Leone, the formation of political parties in the country had its historical basis on a notion of exploitation, greed and political banditry. This has been the case at least since the late 1940s and early 1950s to the present period. It is a status quo that emerged through an unhealthy and insincere struggle for power, which, resultantly, created a dichotomy among the people. It shaped the foundation for the further development of a corrupt middle class that views political power as the license to personal aggrandizement and ultimate access to wealth and prestige in the society. It is a phenomenal development, the result of a colonial social construction, which propelled and heightened a crude contest for power and greedy accumulation of wealth among middle class puppets interested in controlling and maintaining the neocolonial political and economic infrastructure created by British colonizers. The immediate result of such an unhealthy arrangement and its accompanying horizontal contest came at the expense of both ethnographical and geographical cohesion: ethnic and regional fragmentation of the country.

It is this historic desire to exploit and control the national resources of the country that gave birth, through oppressive and deceptive methods, to all other kinds of social contradictions in the country: ethnic divisions, regional fragmentation, political corruptions, economic exploitation and greedy accumulation. The end products include mass poverty, underdevelopment, and the collapse of social institutions, illiteracy, and absence of social services, growing unemployment, low wages and family crisis.

These above conditions are the direct ramifications of the vicious system that functions as a pedestal for imperialist exploitation and oppression. Its real character and functioning is neocolonial in nature and style. It is a system that necessitates the implant and perpetuation of a failed neocolonial class that remains insensitive to addressing the people's problems.

Today the vast majority of the masses in Sierra Leone live in abject poverty despite the abundant resources in the country. Thuggish ruling classes who continue to run a failed neocolonial state are growing extremely rich by living on the blood of the people. They continually hold the rest of the masses hostage to poverty and underdevelopment. Those who are responsible for this chaotic phenomenon are conscious of the penury they inflict on the masses. It is a conscious decision to protect their own class interests – a primitive petty bourgeois interest designed to reap the people for the benefit of a handful of rank opportunists.

Ideological analysis should form basis of the struggle

That is why it is our responsibility to add our voice to this whole debate over a "third force approach" to solving the people's problems. Any serious solution to the problems confronting the country has to have a thorough ideological analysis of the current status quo with a view to helping the people arrive at the understanding of the relationship they have with the system in question. This analysis should not only be based on the simple idea of the people's aspiration for change. But it should have its starting point on the efforts to overturn the existing social system, which is the source of the troubles they continually experience. More importantly, the analysis should also have the potency of presenting a worldview that will help the people to understand the circumstances that necessitated the existence of the system and how other oppressed people around the world are suffering as a consequence of the collective relationship to an international capitalist order that survives from their own oppression and exploitation. It is only through this systematic analysis that we will be able to juxtapose a strategy that will genuinely answer to the people's ever increasing aspiration and desire for freedom from this stagnating system responsible for the miserable conditions they collectively face as a people exploited and oppressed.

Imperialism and neocolonialism create misery

The people should know clearly that this system is not an isolated system but is tied to an international exploiting system referred to as capitalism, which itself became a world system as a consequence of the exploitation and oppression of Africa and African people worldwide. They should equally understand that it is the relationship between them and this international capitalist order or imperialist system that blocks and jeopardizes their struggle for self-determination and, ultimately, snatches away their right to take control of their national resources and decide how they should live or ought to live.

They must also recognize that this process of suppression and or denial of their democratic right to decide how they should live have been made possible by the forceful installation of puppets on the rest of the African world who function exclusively as agents carrying out imperialist decisions and policies in their various communities. It is this international conspiracy, giving support and backing to a rogue middle class, which necessitates the functioning of a neocolonial system serving the interests of imperialism that in turn protects its continuous existence.

Today, the conditions of the people of Sierra Leone, for instance, have worsened and continue to deteriorate at supersonic speed since the British flag was lowered in 1961, raising the question as to whether it was necessary for the country to demand "independence" from Britain. But the truth is that what happened in 1961 was not an event of independence but another transition of power from one group of colonial exploiters to another; the only difference is that Africans were now in control of state affairs but working for the interests of the same imperial power.

Years after that event, the British themselves are visibly in the country running the affairs of the state. The British Department for International Development (DFID) is in charge of deciding whatever economic program is undertaken in the country. The British International Military Advisory Training Team (IMATT) is in charge of restructuring, training and controlling the country's army. The Office of National Security (ONS) is headed and supervised by British military officers; the senior defense adviser to President Ahmed Tejan Kabbah is a British officer; the Deputy Anti-Corruption Commissioner is also British; the Director of Agriculture at the Ministry of Agriculture and Food Security is a British expatriate official; British judges now sit and adjudicate matters in the courts; the British train the police and until recently a British police officer was head of the police; and the Commonwealth Police Training Team was in charge of the police service.

In November 2005, the British government also sent a team to the Sierra Leone Police Training School at Hastings in Freetown to discuss arrangements of direct affiliation with Bradford University in England. This arrangement will allow police officers from Sierra Leone to be sent to England for advanced training whilst at the same time making it necessary for British police officers to come to Sierra Leone under the guise of training the country's police personnel. A British military base had already been created in the country and no one knows the current number of British troops stationed up the Freetown peninsula at Hill Station.

This is being done to provide protection and security for a puppet middle class government which is frantic with fear over the increasing aspiration of the oppressed masses to overturn their suffering by ending the life span of this suffocating system. It is a counter insurgency program designed primarily in response to any efforts by the masses to galvanize themselves in defense of their inalienable right to self-determination.

Third force is not the solution

This is also a clear indication that the so-called "third force" argument is no solution to this political struggle between the mass of ordinary people and the primitive African petty bourgeoisie. The reason for this is that the proponents of the "third force" alternative are themselves sections of the middle class who feel alienated from their compatriots due to the growing power struggle within and among the middle class parties themselves. It is the contest for power and leadership within the various existing middle class parties that led to the emergence of this other group of disgruntled power hungry politicians whose aim is to equally manipulate sufferings and aspirations of the people for genuine change to fulfill their political ambitions and economic motives.

This is exactly what has occurred in the country with the formation or creation of all the political parties in the country, starting from the All Peoples Congress (APC) under Siaka Stevens; to Taimu Bangura's Peoples Democratic Party (PDP); and United National People's Party (UNPP) of Dr. John Kerefa Smarth; Abass Bundu's Peoples Progressive Party (PPP); to Johnny faa Koroma's Peoples Liberation Party (PLP); and the Revolutionary United Front Party (RUFP); and, lately, Charles Margai's Peoples Movement for Democratic Change (PMDC).

The reality is that none of these parties truly represent the country's needs and aspirations for genuine change. And neither of these parties nor their various leaders have political programs that seek to liberate the country from neocolonial and imperialist exploitation and oppression. These parties themselves lack any ideological program that addresses or explains the basis of the poverty and appalling conditions facing the people of the country.

The reason is that the leaders of these parties are themselves members of the class that creates and propels the miserable existence of the masses. And the emergence of these parties, in fact, is a direct result of the increasing power struggle evident among the primitive African petty bourgeoisie as a result of their desperate, vaulting, and ambitious desires to loot and exploit the national wealth. It is this same insincere desire and hidden political agenda that equally led to the production and reproduction of this equivalently similar group of rogues piloting what they describe as "a third force approach" as a final solution to changing the status quo.

The building of another political party made up of disgruntled members of this status quo is no solution to the problems. Rather, it will serve to escalate and worsen the crisis that has been forced upon the people by the numerous contradictions created by neocolonialism and imperialism.

Charles Margai and the Peoples Movement for Democratic Change (PMDC) are the most recent example. The PMDC obviously was born as a consequence of leadership acrimony that wrecked the Sierra Leone Peoples Party (SLPP) in part because of the unwillingness of some party members to continue under the leadership of gerontocracts[5] and the latter's adamancy to create room for new and upcoming leadership.

This being the case, it will be correct to say that Margai would have remained an SLPP member if the party had allowed him to be its leader. Margai's decision to form the PMDC is born primarily from his conclusion that his continuation in the SLPP was a hindrance to his struggle for state power. He had resigned more than once from the party each time he lost in a convention. Consequently, the PMDC is in no way a party that should represent itself to the people as a credible alternative to changing the status quo because its leadership was part of the status quo but opted out of it because they think their selfish political motives cannot be realized within the SLPP and are no longer compatible with those already in power.

---

[5] Herein used to refer to the rule or leadership of old people or the elderly in society.

Third force, a middle class strategy to win power

The "third force approach" is consequently a plot conceived and hatched by the disgruntled sections of the middle class with the sole ambition of manipulating the people in their selfish struggle to seize power for themselves from their opposing middle class compatriots at the very expense of the masses. This has always been a common strategy utilized by those already in power who these "third force" proponents seek to replace through the support of the masses. And the truth is that the middle class political elite is obviously aware of their insignificance and absolutely conscious of their inability to win a struggle without manipulating the people to accomplish their often-selfish desires. Their lack of significance is so obvious that it makes this minute class of individuals vulnerable and insecure without the instruments of coercion.

Real freedom lies in the ability to organize the masses

It is, therefore, essential for the people to understand that this system cannot be changed by replacing one group of middle class individuals with another nor can it be through the creation of a "new party" of some group of self-proclaimed saints who portray themselves as messiahs of the people. The oppressed masses must organize themselves into a political organization of their own; one that is made up of the oppressed and exploited masses and represents their interests through a general program for the future. By this it is meant that they have to build and be part of an organization that has the ability, strength and capacity to lead a struggle for self-determination by ultimately fulfilling their aspirations to be free from neocolonialism and imperialism. This is primarily important because the struggle for self-determination falls within the general effort to overturn a social system consciously imposed by imperialism and is, consequently, the source of all miserable conditions facing oppressed people across the globe. It is only through the building of such a political organization that they will ultimately take the path that will lead to a coherent approach of how they can collectively end their suffering and regain control of their fundamental right to become a self-governing people. In the final analysis, it is only through such a process that the primitive African petty bourgeoisie will be destroyed—a process which equally means the defeat of imperialism and restoration of the right to self-determination to the oppressed. That is the collective task of all oppressed people in Sierra Leone.

CHAPTER 2

SOCIALISM, DEMOCRACY AND NATIONAL DEVELOPMENT

In November 2009, the Africanist Movement convened a three-day consultative conference at the British Council Hall in Freetown, Sierra Leone. The conference, which was held from November 16-18, 2009, was part of the movement's plan to build a revolutionary party in Sierra Leone that will contest against the existing middle class parties in the country for control of state power. The three-day conference attended by more than six hundred delegates and international observers resolved to transform the Africanist Movement into a socialist party. At the conclusion of the conference, an interim leadership committee was formed under the leadership of Chernoh Alpha M. Bah. The Committee's task was to convene the first congress of a socialist party in Sierra Leone a year later. But a few days after this development, the new socialist organization was attacked by sections of the political elite and its press officers. The Torchlight Newspaper in Freetown took the lead in this offensive when the newspaper's editor, Mohamed Sankoh, published an editorial in the paper describing the newly established socialist committee as a group of jokers. The newspaper claimed that Sierra Leone's underdevelopment was the result of puerile socialist policies implemented by the All Peoples Congress (APC) during the 1970s and 1980s. The newspaper, owned by an official of the ruling party, concluded that socialism will not resolve the country's problem. In the following article, therefore, Chernoh Alpha M. Bah not only responds to the accusations against the leadership of the African Socialist Movement but also exposes the fact that the APC's claim to socialism is false and that the poverty and underdevelopment of the country are the result of capitalist driven programs. The article asserts that socialism can only occur in Sierra Leone with the advent of the African Socialist Movement.

"...Sierra Leone under former president Siaka Stevens once tested that socialism road. Albeit president Stevens did not openly declare this country a socialist state, most if not all of his policies had their roots in socialism...the corruption that permeated the political landscape of that time showed that socialism as a system of governance would never be a panacea for this country's political salvation....the half-assed socialist policies of Siaka Stevens which were continued by ex-president Joseph Saidu Momoh are some of the reasons why this country is at present in a pretty prickle..."[6]

These are exact words from an article written by Mohamed Sankoh of the pro-All Peoples Congress (APC) *Torchlight Newspaper* in Freetown. Sankoh's aim was to criticize the newly formed Interim Committee of the African Socialist Movement (ASM) of Sierra Leone, which he described as an enterprise of "jokers" and "conmen" that are working to attract financing from some socialist quarters in Latin America.

While the entire article centered on self-contradictory opinion from the writer, it is also a piece of literature that evidently lacks the required facts and intellectual basis to convince anyone.

At any rate, it is our responsibility to help rectify the many confused notions that Sankoh and his friends in the All Peoples Congress (APC) seek to sell to the people of Sierra Leone. In particular, it is appropriate for us to examine some of the misleading nuances that emerge from the said critique of the movement and, equally so, the whole question of socialism in Sierra Leone as put forward by the African Socialist Movement.

It is obvious that Sankoh's position – mirroring that of the many APC leaders and members that the *Torchlight Newspaper*[7] represents – is not only misleading and faulty. It is equally part of an endeavor to validate and mask the failures of middle class political elites whose policies, programs and activities have produced all the miserable conditions experienced in Sierra Leone. Sankoh's article was obviously defending a group whose political decisions for over fifty years has ruined and is still ruining the country's potential for growth and development. The task before us now is to examine Sankoh's misleading argument that the crisis and social contradictions produced by the more than two decades of one-party dictatorship by the APC was a consequence of some socialist policies and programs of past APC leaders.

Sankoh says in his own words that the "country is at present in a pretty prickle" because of some "half-assed socialist policies" of Siaka Stevens, which in his opinion, were continued by Joseph Momoh. The questions arising from

---

[6] Mohamed Sankoh (2009). *A Joke Called the African Socialist Movement.* Torchlight Newspapers, Freetown (November 25, 2009) p3

[7] The *Torchlight Newspaper* is owned by Sheka Tarawalie, the Press Secretary to President Ernest Koroma in 2007, who was later, promoted to a Deputy Minister first in the Information Ministry and then transferred to the Internal Affairs Ministry.

this position are too many: what were the policies of Siaka Stevens and Joseph Momoh that Mohamed Sankoh describes as half-assed socialist policies? And how did these so-called half-assed socialist policies result in the pretty prickle that Sankoh refers to? On what basis and circumstances did Mohamed Sankoh refer to these two APC leaders – Siaka Stevens and Joseph Momoh – as socialists? Is the failure of Stevens and Momoh a failure of socialism or a failure of the APC as a party? Also, how does the failure of the APC relate to the formation of the African Socialist Movement of Sierra Leone?

It is the answers to these questions that will help us to equally understand whether Siaka Stevens and, ultimately, the All Peoples Congress, of which he was the main brain, were truly socialist. It is also these questions that will help us to understand the true meaning of socialism and the underlying differences between the African Socialist Movement of Sierra Leone and the other ethnic-centered, regionalist middle class factions currently masquerading as political parties in the country.

Siaka Stevens: a political opportunist, not a socialist

Siaka Stevens, like some other dishonest African politicians of the 1960s, was a political opportunist and was nowhere near being a socialist of any description. Regardless of the fact that Siaka Stevens infrequently referred to himself and the APC as socialists, there was no evidence of any kind of socialism, or the likelihood of it, in Siaka Stevens or the APC itself. This fact is stated clearly in the APC's book, *The Rising Sun*, which observed categorically that "…the APC party in Sierra Leone can claim to be one of the very few in Africa, indeed in the developing world, which has not fallen into the trap of professing an ideology, much less of committing itself to a policy determined by theoretical considerations…"[8]

In 1967 the APC also emphatically stated in paragraph two of its *Manifesto* that it does not believe in a socialist revolution, but it is advocating for an "evolution," and that its activities are inspired by pragmatism, which the APC also said was "incompatible with faith or adherence to an ideology."

Siaka Stevens himself stated clearly, during his address to the 3rd National Delegates Conference of the APC held at Brookfields Stadium in May of 1970, stated, "the foreign policy of the APC government is one of non-alignment." Besides, Stevens openly rejected nine years later at the Commonwealth Prime Ministers and Heads of State Conference held in Lusaka, Zambia in August of 1979 the idea that his APC government was a proxy or ally of the Chinese Communist Party or some other socialist country.

With all this evidence, it is questionable how Mohamed Sankoh arrived at the conclusion that the failure of the APC under Siaka Stevens and Joseph Momoh

---

[8] See Page 254 of *The Rising Sun* published by the All Peoples Congress (APC). Additional information on this question can also be found in *What Life Has Taught Me* by Siaka Stevens.

was due to some socialist policy when Stevens, in particular, and the APC, in general, had stated openly that they were never socialists in the first place?

Yes, it is obvious that for dishonest political reasons, Stevens and some of the earlier generation of the APC cadre of the 1960s occasionally branded themselves as socialists. There were occasions when Siaka Stevens referred to himself and his party as socialist. This is why I say without hesitation and with confidence that Stevens and the APC he founded were a bunch of political opportunists. They used and misused the terminology of socialism to satisfy their selfish and opportunistic political tendencies and aspirations.

It is obvious that following the ideological contest that emerged after 1945 between the Soviet Union and the United States, several opportunist leaders in Africa and elsewhere took it upon themselves to exploit the race for national proxies among the imperialist powers. Stevens, like several others, played into this situation, hence his relationship with the Chinese and Cubans.

This is, however, no justification that Stevens or the APC was socialist and had experimented with socialism in Sierra Leone. There is a vast difference between a self-proclaimed individual socialist in power and when socialism is actually in power. It is misleading to speak of socialism or a socialist state when the workers and peasants are not in control of power. The workers and peasants cannot come to power independent of a revolutionary workers party that provides leadership for their struggle to break free from the chains of capitalist exploitation and greed.

The APC was never founded as a revolutionary workers party and neither did it introduce a program that has anything to do with a worker-peasant struggle for power in the name of a socialist revolution in the history of politics in Sierra Leone. In fact, the APC of Siaka Stevens was opposed to the idea of a socialist revolution, and there are no guesses about this. The seemingly socialist terminology that permeated the ranks of the APC cadre of the 1960s was not the result of some socialist conclusions on the part of Stevens but, in large part, due to the influence of Wallace-Johnson and his relationship to Stevens.

Wallace-Johnson, of course, was the most outstanding advocate for workers' rights and the first to have raised – through the West African Youth League – the question of socialism in Sierra Leone and the centrality of young people in the political future of West Africa. Although Stevens was evidently influenced by the trade union skills and organizing qualities of Wallace-Johnson, his sudden rise in the trade union movement and eventually the political terrain of Sierra Leone was consequently the result of the colonialist's defeat of Wallace-Johnson and the West African Youth League in the late 1930s. Stevens, in particular, received a scholarship to Ruskin's College as a direct beneficiary of the British strategy to de-radicalize the militant tendency and anti-imperialist stance of the Sierra Leone trade union movement then influenced by the conclusions of Wallace-Johnson.

This is why some political historians have concluded that there was no genuine anti-imperialist struggle in Sierra Leone since the defeat of the West African Youth League, and there has never been an attempt towards socialism in the country after Wallace-Johnson. Therefore, to blame the failure of the APC on socialism of whatever sort is like trying to teach College mathematics to a kindergarten student.

Stevens: a tool for the IMF, World Bank

It is obvious that the social contradictions that plunged Sierra Leone into the crisis that the country is still struggling to recover from today were the direct ramifications of the neoliberal, capitalist driven policies and programs of the APC first under Stevens and then Joseph Momoh.

It was the IMF and World Bank Structural Adjustment Programs (SAPs) of the 1970s and 1980s, implemented by the APC, that bankrupted the economy and created massive unemployment, price instability, infrastructural decline, heightened poverty and the collapse of all social institutions in the country. The IMF and World Bank Structural Adjustment Programs were surely not motivated by any tendency towards socialism by Stevens or Momoh. They were not produced by any socialist tendency or project. They were part of a whole array of imperialist-designed economic programs and policies conceived to promote the capitalist world economy.

It was results of these capitalist-driven programs and intervention from international financial institutions that plunged Sierra Leone into devastating conflict. It was the economic difficulties and collapse of social institutions that resulted from the IMF and World Bank regulated policies of the APC, which created the basis for the many student uprisings of the 1970s and 1980s, respectively. It was the hardship, which resulted from these capitalist-driven policies that radicalized Fourah Bay College students leading to their stoning of Siaka Stevens during a University convocation ceremony at Mount Aureol. It was also acute economic difficulty created by neoliberal, capitalist economic policies that forced the APC of Siaka Stevens to introduce the forceful culture of neocolonial dictatorship that enforced a tactic of repression and political intolerance unprecedented in Sierra Leone.

Again, it was Siaka Stevens' capitalist policies that gave out the lucrative diamond mines of Kono and Tongo fields in the east of the country to British-controlled corporations and exploitative Lebanese businessmen depriving the people of Sierra Leone of the resources required for their own meaningful existence. It is unquestionable that Siaka Stevens was definitely a tool of the IMF and World Bank who worked overtime to satisfy the interests of western capitalist corporations and Lebanese businesses at the expense of the progress and development of Sierra Leone. It was the failure and rebounding impacts of the APC's one party neocolonial dictatorship of Stevens and Momoh that resulted into the RUF rebellion of Foday Sankoh.

Sierra Leone has never witnessed socialism

It is massively erroneous to state that the APC or Siaka Stevens started off as socialists. There has never been socialism in Sierra Leone under the APC of Stevens or Momoh. Neither has there been a political party in Sierra Leone that is or was expressly a socialist party both in theory and practice. All available data from the APC records attest to this overwhelming truth. Even where claims of socialism appeared to have been advanced by some APC members and leaders, there also exist abundant material and evidence that invalidate such assertions. The APC or Siaka Stevens were never socialists and did not experiment with socialism, as put forward by Mohamed Sankoh and his APC friends.

The fact is that there will be no socialism in Sierra Leone without a socialist transformation. And a socialist transformation is possible only through a struggle that will allow the workers in alliance with the peasants to assume control of state power. This will happen only through the development of a revolutionary workers party: a socialist party with a program that addresses the needs and aspirations of the workers and peasants to overcome the social contradictions imposed on them by the class contradictions of neocolonialism and capitalist imperialism.

This was never the case with the APC or Siaka Stevens. The political and historical circumstances that led to the emergence of Siaka Stevens and the APC were as spontaneous and opportunistic as the same circumstances that introduced a shabby discourse on socialism within the ranks of the APC during the 1960s. Both were generally the by-products of political dishonesty generated by the vaulting ambition of the APC leadership rather than a nationalistic fervor or some commitment to popular democracy on their part.

For instance, how can we explain the fact that Siaka Stevens, who noted in Paragraph 3 of the 1967 APC Manifesto that "...the SLPP government of Margai has attempted to introduce one party rule in this freedom-loving country and has gone to the extent of telling the country that it wants to force an unacceptable and tyrannical Republican constitution down our throats..." could equally be the catalyst for the introduction of the repulsive one-party dictatorship in Sierra Leone and the protagonist for the imprisonment of all democratic potentials in the country? This is nothing but political dishonesty and caustic banditry.

Petty Bourgeois, Philistine Attitude

It is good to write and publish one's thoughts and opinions. But it will be theoretically reckless to just write and publish inconsistent views simply because one seems to have access to empty newspaper pages. No matter how subjective a journalist tends to be, he or she should ensure that whatever theoretical positions put out in a newspaper or journal should be one that could be easily defended with corresponding facts and information.

But it appeared that Mohamed Sankoh ignored this basic literary principle, and, in the process, he manifested what could be referred to as a petty-bourgeois, philistine attitude. This is especially the case with his treatment of the question of workers and peasants.

He said without any data to substantiate his point that "…this country has always been betrayed by the very workers and peasants…" And he went further to name Siaka Stevens, Momoh, Paul Koroma and Tejan Kabbah as examples of workers who have held power in Sierra Leone. To further add garbage into already muddy water, Sankoh used the 2002 Edition of the Oxford English Dictionary as his guide in defining both the workers and peasants and, also, socialism itself.

As regards peasants, he said they are "an ignorant, rude or unsophisticated" people. This is not only a shallow definition of peasants, but it typifies a complete disdain for peasants by bourgeois academics. It is only the philistine attitude of bourgeois intellectualism that lumps workers or peasants into the category of "unsophisticated" or some other derogatory terminology like those found in Mohamed Sankoh's article. This is complete intellectual absurdity.

The questions are these: are professors or academics the ones who create value or is value created by workers and peasants? If all value in society is produced by the very workers and peasants, then why are workers or peasants regarded by bourgeois intellectuals as "ignorant, rude and unsophisticated" group?

In today's world, theories are being advanced on a daily basis, and many theoretical advancements have taken place during the last one hundred years that have answered some of the most problematic ideological and theoretical questions of the day. Writers like Walter Rodney, Franz Fanon, Cheik Anta Diop, Kwame Nkrumah and Amilcar Cabral answered many of these questions years ago. There is abundant literature to be referenced on issues like these rather than limiting oneself to a dictionary phrase that passes as a definition of an ideological concept or a whole political theory.

Socialism is popular democracy

This is the same approach adopted by the thinking representatives of the capitalist world when discussing the question of democracy. It is not rare to see bourgeois academics attempting to discuss democracy as a contrast to socialism but make capitalism synonymous with democracy. They draw parallels between capitalism and democracy as if the two are compatibles and they equate socialism with despotism and tyranny.

The African Socialist Movement, in particular, has stated that the struggle for socialism in Sierra Leone is a struggle for *popular democracy*. It will be difficult to talk of *real democracy* in a situation where only a handful of old politicians – almost an insignificant two percent of the population – have created legislations and institutions that imprison the vast majority to their political dictates and wishes. This is not democracy but a dictatorship of an aristocracy that is falsely legalized with the adjectives of democracy.

The struggle of the workers and peasants to assume control of the state is a struggle aimed at liberating the vast majority of the population from the chains of neocolonialist dictatorship that has impoverished the greater proportion of the masses. In the final analysis, it is only through the rule and mandate of the majority – the workers and peasants - that we will be able to experience the fruits of a *real democracy*. And this is only possible under socialism where the majority will be in control of power and the right to decision making. Democracy is inseparable with socialism. It is intellectually fraudulent and politically dishonest to attempt to disconnect democracy from socialism.

Socialism possible in Sierra Leone with ASM

This socialism is a possibility in Sierra Leone only with the African Socialist Movement (ASM). The ASM, apart from being the first socialist formation in the recent history of the country, has created the opportunity for a socialist transformation to occur in Sierra Leone. The historical and political basis for this to happen has manifested emphatically with the formation of the ASM.

The ASM undoubtedly presents an opportunity – for the first time in the current history of the country – to African workers and poor peasants to challenge the politically blemished and suffocating middle class politicians in Sierra Leone who have sold out the country's resources and future to a consortium of capitalist nations and imperialist organizations.

With a revolutionary national democratic program that calls for nationalization of strategic sectors of the economy, expansion of the public service, increase in minimum wage and better conditions of service, an agrarian program for farmers, youth employment and provision of social services to better the conditions of life of the people, the ASM is breaking the usual narrow politics of ethnicism of the middle class politicians of the APC, SLPP and PMDC.

Through the discourse on socialism, the ASM introduces an issue-oriented program into the political terrain that gives voice to the aspirations and desires of the workers and peasants. These sectors of the population have always had their energies and strengths selfishly exploited for over fifty years now by the APC and SLPP combined. In the final analysis, it is the struggle of the advanced sector of this exploited class to become the new ruling class that will unravel and expose the political treachery and dishonesty of the neocolonialist leaders and parties currently in power in Sierra Leone and other parts of the African world.

In fact, Sierra Leone can only harness the potentials of development with the actualization of a worker-peasant government. This is the only process that will allow for the workers and peasants – the vast majority of the population – to be in control of state power and change their material conditions of existence.

CHAPTER 3

THE ETHNIC AND CITIZENSHIP QUESTION IN AFRICA:

A CASE OF FULAS IN SIERRA LEONE

*In early 2009, a group of activists and academics attempted to undertake a debate on the question of ethnicity and tribal divide in Africa. The debate, organized on the online discussion forum of the Freedom of Information Coalition of Sierra Leone (FOISL), was motivated by desires from members of the Forum to investigate the root causes of the social division created by tribalism or ethnicity and how this could be resolved. The following article, which was later published by the **Africanist Bulletin**, is Chernoh Alpha M. Bah's contribution to the debate. In this article, Chernoh Alpha M. Bah argues that the ethnic divisions in Africa are a legacy of colonialism, and they present a question of citizenship that could be addressed through an honest political initiative that requires an objective recognition of the problem as its affects minorities on the continent. To understand the problem, one has to wear the lenses of so-called "minority ethnic groups" and feel directly how they are affected by the actions of the supposedly "established majority groups." In Sierra Leone, Chernoh Alpha M. Bah argues in the ensuing article that this can best be understood by examining the situation of Fula people and their struggle for "equality rights" or "citizenship" in Sierra Leone.*

It is of course true that "tribalism", "ethnicity", "racism" or whatever name it assumes is a major cancer that has poisoned the unity and development of Africa. This is a social contradiction that manifests itself separately and differently across the continent. And while every African, including our intellectuals themselves, would always lambaste ethnicists, they too are often ethnic-segregationists at heart. Most dangerously, they often raise the ethnic question and play its card only when they are at a losing end of some national contest.

We can only fully understand the nature of this contradiction and the ways to handle it if we approach it from the general question of citizenship and its accompanying relatives. I hold the opinion that it is only through a dialectical examination of the question of citizenship, especially as it relates to equitable access to national resources and protection from the state, that we will fully appreciate and understand the corrosive dangers of ethnicity and its divisions, and what possible measures could be adopted to harmonize the existing antagonisms that have resulted from these divides. We can take the Fula[9] people of Sierra Leone as an example to study the dimensions of ethnic marginalization on the African continent. The Fula community in Sierra Leone could be regarded as a set of African people that has suffered from the negative and divisive impacts of this cancerous social phenomenon called "tribalism" or "ethnicism" in Sierra Leone.

I have chosen to deal with this discussion from the perspective of my association with the Fula community and also my own individual experiences. While the conclusion drawn from such an analysis faces the risk of entrapment by factors of subjectivity, my personal position on this matter could also help inform the underlying currents presented by such a divisive situation.

I would hasten to say that throughout my life in Sierra Leone, despite the fact that all my parents and myself were all born in Sierra Leone, I still have had to struggle, even with the most educated in the country, to prove each time that I have the same rights of "belongingness" as Temnes, Limbas, Mendes or any other community of African people in the country.

This is why I believe discussing the ethnic problem in Sierra Leone without reference to this situation represents an unfair analysis. When I go around Sierra Leone, I often hear talk of national unity and ethnic cohesion, mostly sprouted by political party leaders desperately looking for votes. But beneath this lie a silence and a yet "un-expressed" feeling of xenophobia, despite the fact that most of our brothers and sisters often tell you that Sierra Leone is the freest country in the world. My response to this statement is that it has often been the complete opposite.

I hold the view that our people are among the most xenophobically minded people in Africa. The only helpful thing for now is that they have never had the opportunity to demonstrate and unleash that colossal innate feeling of xenophobia.

For instance, over the last three years I have received abundant complaints from numerous Fula people—who are unquestionable citizens of the country—that

---

[9] The Fulas, also known as *Peul* in Guinea and *Fulani* in Nigeria, are a major ethnic group in West Africa. They are found in almost every country across West Africa. They refer to themselves as *fulbe* in some areas and speak a language called *pular*. In Sierra Leone, they are among the earliest groups of settlers in that territory. They are part of the sixteen ethnic groups in Sierra Leone, and are arguably today the third largest ethnic group.

their passport applications were being deliberately rejected by the Immigration Department. I do not want to state here my own individual experience with immigration officials in Freetown during my application for a passport.

In May 2007, I was forced to intervene when a cousin of mine, who was about to travel to the United States for advanced studies, had her passport application rejected. When I went to the Immigration Department, I was told that Madam Alice Kamara, who was then head of immigration, was requesting that the applicant's father should appear for an interview to prove his citizenship; otherwise, the daughter would not be issued a passport. I found it preposterous and insulting because the same procedure never applied to other ethnic groups. And to my dismay, I discovered that there were hundreds of other Fula people whose applications had suffered the same fate. I became enraged when the immigration staff showed me tons of application forms—over four hundred of them all bearing Fula names— rejected on ethnic considerations: just because they were Fulas. It showed a clear attempt to single out Fulas from the rest of the other African masses in the country by the immigration department.

I reported the issue to several senior members of the Fula community in Freetown but no action was taken. Later, I was informed that those applying have to be certified by the Fula tribal head in Freetown, who is required to send a letter of confirmation to the Immigration Department attesting that the applicant qualifies for a passport. This also was a procedure for the Fulas only, and it did not apply to any other ethnic group. Personally, I met Alice Kamara while she was head of immigration to have a first-hand explanation of the situation. As always, she appeared saint-like, offering flimsy legal explanations and denying that it was a witch-hunt on the part of the authorities against the Fulas. I suggested to Alice Kamara and some of the officials present that the issue be made a public debate, but she declined on the grounds that it would have to be approved by Dr. Ahmed Tejan Kabbah, who was then president of the country.

But this is not only a problem with the immigration department; the question of citizenship and the right of Fula people to co-exist and have equitable access to state resources, just like any other set of African people in Sierra Leone, is one that has always remained controversial and displeasing to many within the corridors of power and some of their supporters on the streets. This includes members of the Fula middle class who have benefited from the daily struggles of the common Fula people to gain their basic democratic rights as citizens in a multi-ethnic and multi-religious country.

This does not imply that we do not have people with Fula names like Dr. Minkailu Bah and others who today occupy significant positions across the country, but they appear afraid or silent when issues of nationality and citizenship are raised. Even when they comment, they chose to do so inoffensively in street corners and in their sitting rooms or during their prayer sessions. They are afraid to come public because they always think there is much they could lose.

It is my view that, it is no mystery that Fula peoples have been historically oppressed in Sierra Leone, yet some would try to deny this fact based on political and intellectual dishonesty. The situation of Fula people in Sierra Leone is one that is shrouded with controversy only because of this insincerity. The idea that led the Fula's suffering ethnic persecution is an artificial construction that was nurtured in the 1960s and crudely accentuated in the 1970s by the All Peoples Congress (APC) government of Siaka Stevens. The older generation of Fulas, who are living witnesses to the xenophobic treatments they experienced during those bitter days of the APC, now appear to be comfortable with the few ministerial appointments that recent governments, especially the past Sierra Leone Peoples Party (SLPP) government of Kabbah, bestowed on people with Fula names, but these individuals are of no real good to the interests of the suffering, uneducated Fulas enduring the pain of daily police extortion and caustic ethnicism from other members of the communities in which they reside.

The question is whether these few nominal ministerial posts and other appointments are enough to erase the often familiar "apartheid-like" mistreatment they suffered from the hands and feet of red-beret police officers of the APC whose duties were to identify, publicly humiliate and coagulate Fulas in police stations for the single reason that a political group refuses to accept their right to undisputed nationality or citizenship.

These so-called Fula ministers, lawyers and parliamentarians of today appear unmoved even when their kith and kin are still publicly embarrassed. It has always been the youthful sector of the community, experiencing this daily shocking embarrassment from this system of power, that always agitates for its rightful status and place in the country.

So if we are serious about eroding tribalism and the ethnic divide that is seemingly devastating the much-needed unity required for national growth and development, we should situate the discourse on this matter on the general question of citizenship—a discourse on citizenship that is not only limited to the right to carry a passport, but one that allows for the existence of a social equilibrium that guarantees the right to share and collectively exist without primacy of one group over another.

Let me emphasize that I am not an ethic nationalist or "tribal patriot". I am a Pan-Africanist and a socialist revolutionary that believes in internationalism. My political philosophy and understanding of African history rejects the question of ethnicity as the basis of identification and social existence. Like Kwame Nkrumah stated: "the clan is the extended family and the tribe is the extended clan" and these differences have in pre-colonial times served to strengthen the existence of African people.

"Tribalism" or the hostile ethnic divisions, as they exist today in African communities, are a product of the colonial situation and one that is used to further weaken the unity of the oppressed and exploited African masses by putting them against each other. It is this colonial divide-and-rule tactic that is responsible for the crisis situations most of the "post-colonial" micro states within the continent face today.

Throughout Africa today, the citizenship question has not been addressed in a holistic fashion that allows for the consolidation of the shattered African nation. The pictures of the Rwandan genocide are still fresh in the minds of the African people, and we cannot afford to create a situation that provides nothing but an opportunity for internecine warfare. We are one African people sharing the same historical situation and experiencing the same conditions, whether we are Temnes, Limbas, Mendes or Fulas. It is the collective responsibility of everyone to challenge every attempt by a few individuals, mostly in power, to benefit from the disunity of the masses. This is why I hold the position that we begin this discourse from an examination of the question of citizenship itself. This is my reading on this matter and my individual opinion on the question of ethnicity and citizenship in Africa. As stated earlier, I have deliberately chosen the Fula community in Sierra Leone to help illustrate the nature and character of this social contradiction. It is my hope that the comments expressed so far, albeit subjective but factual, offer a genuine premise for additional debate on this question.

CHAPTER 4

CREOLE NATIONALISM AND WALLACE-JOHNSON'S LEGACY

*Isaac Theophilus Akuna Wallace-Johnson is one of Africa's early trade union organizers. Born in Sierra Leone to parents of freed African slaves called the "Creoles", Wallace-Jonson built one of the most popular mass movements in the history of British colonial West Africa. His sharp criticism of British colonialism and its mining policies created immense problems for British colonial officials. Recognized as the father of trade unionism in Sierra Leone, Wallace-Johnson's influence as an anti-colonial organizer in West Africa was phenomenal and remarkable. He was deported from the Gold Coast (now Ghana) and Nigeria by British colonial officials because of his anti-colonial work. Back in Sierra Leone, his West African Youth League (WAYL) was the first organization that attempted to break the regional divide that had been nurtured by the British colonialists by enlisting members from both the colony and protectorate. The British immediately considered Wallace-Johnson a significant threat to their imperialist grip in West Africa. The British were offended when his West African Youth League (WAYL) won the Freetown City Council elections in 1938. Wallace-Johnson was arrested a few months later and imprisoned on fake emergency orders. Today, much of the history of the West African Youth League (WAYL) and Wallace-Johnson himself has been swept under the carpet of history. Little is known in the country about the great work of this anti-colonial figure. In this article, Chernoh Alpha M. Bah extols the work and vision of Wallace-Johnson, drawing a connection between the work of the West African Youth League and the African Socialist Movement (formerly Africanist Movement). Bah points out that the work of the African Socialist Movement (ASM) is a legacy of the West African Youth League and represents a continuation of the vision of Wallace-Johnson. The article also faults the Creole middle class for burying the work and significance of Wallace-Johnson. This article was published in 2008 by **Africa News** ahead of the Freetown City Council elections in Sierra Leone.*

This year (2008) marks seventy years since the West African Youth League (WAYL)[10] contested and won the Freetown City Council elections in 1938. Wallace-Johnson, founder and leader of the League, died forty-three years ago in a mysterious car crash while attending a worker's conference in Accra, Ghana.

Unfortunately, the West African Youth League, the first anti-colonial mass movement in West Africa that demanded the total and unconditional independence of Africa from European colonial domination, has largely been forgotten. With branches in Ghana, Nigeria and Sierra Leone, the League expressed a working class platform tied to an all-African state power that threatened the ability of British colonialism to continue its direct control and subjugation of what was then British West Africa.

Wallace-Johnson: threat to European colonialism

The early decades of the 20th century saw serious resistance to international capitalism by the colonized masses, causing immense disorder for European colonialism. During this period, Wallace-Johnson became a severe threat to European colonialism in West Africa when he campaigned vigorously against European orchestrated imperialist wars around the world and the spread of nuclear weapons on the continent. He traveled across the region tirelessly organizing against colonial domination and, as West Africa's most prominent trade unionist and political organizer in the 1920s to 1940s, he typified an internationalist whose desire for a liberated, united African people endeared him to the poor and exploited workers of the world struggling against international capitalism and the colonial system responsible for the oppression and exploitation of the world's peoples.

By 1938, the West African Youth League claimed a membership 40,000 strong in Freetown and the provinces of Sierra Leone, empowering it to contest for seats on the Freetown City Council.[11]

Following the victory of the League in the elections, the British became so afraid of Wallace-Johnson's popularity that he was imprisoned and confined throughout the course of the second imperialist war. Upon his release in 1944, he discovered that the League had fragmented, having been "disarmed" by the British colonialists following his imprisonment.

---

[10] Wallace-Johnson founded the West African Youth League in 1935. For a comprehensive narrative see: Spitzer, Leo; Denzer, LaRay (1973a), "I. T. A. Wallace-Johnson and the West African Youth League", *The International Journal of African Historical Studies* (Vol. 6, No. 3) 6 (3): 413–452

[11] The Youth League candidate was Constance Cummings-John. She won a landslide victory and became the first woman mayor in British colonial West Africa.

Setback for African liberation

The Africanist Movement views the imprisonment of Wallace-Johnson as a setback to the African liberation movement in Sierra Leone and West Africa. It is now clear that Wallace-Johnson's imprisonment was part of a larger scheme to undermine the development of the West African Youth League into a movement capable of providing revolutionary leadership to the masses. The destruction of Wallace-Johnson's progressive leadership created space that allowed middle class opportunists to surface as leaders of the "pro-independence" movements that emerged after 1945 in Sierra Leone. Bankole Bright and other "Creole elites" assumed leadership of pseudo anti-colonial movements in the colony and remained opposed to Wallace-Johnson. They also engaged in a struggle with the conservative political elites of the protectorate for control of the neo-colonial state that had been carved out by British colonialists.

The political fragmentations experienced today are a direct result of the unhealthy, selfish and horizontally violent political struggles among these middle class groups. And it is as a consequence of this British neocolonialist strategy, commencing with the defeat of Wallace-Johnson, which created the divide between the colony and the protectorate and later snowballed into the north-west versus south-east alliances of today.

Creole middle class obscures Wallace-Johnson's work

Why is it that the historical and political significance of Wallace-Johnson is not emphasized in our many political discussions that take place in this country? It is my view that the concealment of the significance of Wallace-Johnson and the West African Youth League is due to the political and intellectual dishonesty of the middle class Creole political elites and intellectuals who promote Bankole Bright as the representative of the genuine aspirations of the Creole community in Freetown. Contrarily, Wallace Johnson's quest for undiluted African unity and internationalism superseded ethnic patriotism and individual gratification. "Creole historians" deliberately failed to do justice to Wallace-Johnson's legacy partly because of their own selfish class aspirations and interests. In other words, they shamelessly sacrificed Wallace-Johnson's great work in the pursuit of personal aggrandizement and material gain. For example, the late Prof. Akintola Wyse enjoyed fame resulting from the many sleepless nights spent travelling to-and-from conferences and speaking engagements in Europe and America, where he endorsed reactionaries like Bankole Bright to the detriment of real heroes like Wallace-Johnson. It is this Creole middle class tendency to obscure the relevance of Wallace-Johnson and his great work that gave birth to the philosophy of Creole nationalism, which is today responsible for the contradictions currently bedeviling the Creole community in Freetown around the questions of nationality and identity.

Creole nationalism is a reactionary philosophy

Consequently, we in the Africanist Movement hold the view that Creole nationalism is in no way synonymous with African patriotism and is antithetical to the struggle for the liberation of Africans from the yoke of colonialism. Creole nationalism is a tendency of the Creole middle class elite that is anchored in the reactionary stance of Bankole Bright. The philosophy of Creole nationalism is the product of the egoistic inclinations of the Creole intellectual elites that are arrayed against the true and genuine aspirations of the African working class found in Wallace-Johnson.

Wallace-Johnson was a trade unionist, a journalist and internationalist whose legacy triumphs over the warped philosophy of reactionary intellectual politicians whose struggle for personal aggrandizement, wealth, privilege and status denies them the opportunity of standing on the right side of history. It rises above the waffled, unprincipled head-over-heels approach to politics found in the thoughts and actions of power thirsty hustlers. Creole middle class opportunism has buried the defiant spirit and progressive leadership of Wallace-Johnson and has betrayed the rightful role and place of the "Creole community" in the genuine struggle for the emancipation of the African from centuries of oppression and exploitation.

Africanist Movement anchored on Wallace-Johnson's legacy

Now, seventy years later, we in the Africanist Movement have taken on the task of forwarding the legacy of the West African Youth League by contesting the upcoming local government elections as part of our strategy to unite and liberate our people under an all-African socialist state. We are lifting up Wallace-Johnson and his defiant spirit as a shining, valuable example for the people in our struggle for a better future. The Africanist Movement proudly embodies the spirit of Wallace-Johnson and carries on the legacy of the West African Youth League as a barometer in our struggle for state power. It is a struggle to rectify the limitations inherent in the League and to call into question the betrayal of Wallace-Johnson by middle class opportunists whose view on political power did not go beyond the desire to selfishly advance their status and prestige at the expense of the welfare of the poor masses.

Raising Wallace-Johnson disarms his critics

Critics have often pointed to the disintegration of the West African Youth League as evidence of Wallace-Johnson's inexperience and failed political strategy rather than the result of repressive colonial politics accelerated by the collaborative treachery of the middle class. The resurrection of the defiant spirit and valuable work of Wallace-Johnson disarms his critics and, by implication, represents a threat to the existing deceitfulness of the middle class. They are exposed and rendered powerless, defenseless and feeble when confronted with struggle of the African working class for self-determination. This collective understanding is shared by members of the Africanist Movement and should occupy a central position in the political and historical discourses of our time. We remain proud that, seventy years on, history still vindicates Wallace-Johnson and his legacy continues to thrive.

PART II
COMBATING NEOCOLONIALISM:
THE INTERNAL CONTRADICTIONS

CHAPTER 5

ELIMINATING "INTER-COMMUNAL VIOLENCE" IN AFRICA

The following is an excerpt from a speech presented by Chernoh Alpha M. Bah at the Reconciliation, Reparations, Repatriation and Transformation Conference held at the University of Ghana-Legon, Accra, Ghana from 24th -27th July, 2006. The event was organized by the National Coalition of Blacks for Reparations in America (NCOBRA)'s International Affairs Commission, USA and SUCARDIF Association of Ghana.

On behalf of the Africanist Movement, I wish to express our profound appreciation to all of you for inviting us to this historically significant event. First, I will tell you something about the Africanist Movement of which I am the Director. The Africanist Movement is an independent mass organization founded five years ago in Sierra Leone with the uncompromising aim of fighting for the liberation and unification of Africa and African people. We believe in the oneness of Africa and acknowledge the similar conditions and contradictions that African people face wherever we live.

Today, our movement boasts a membership of seventy thousand African youth throughout West Africa who are determined to overturn the conditions we confront as a consequence of the parasitic activities of capitalism. As a revolutionary organization, we maintain that freedom given by the oppressor is fraudulent. Consequently we are committed to fighting for genuine freedom. Our movement is now engaged in efforts to build a singular international organization committed to organizing Africans worldwide to fight for the freedom and unification of Africa and African people.

I am also here to talk about "Strategies for Eliminating Inter-Communal Violence on the African Continent." We all know the conditions that African people experience around the globe; war, famine, disease, declining economies, chaos and numerous social problems that can be attributed to neocolonial state repression, bad governance, mismanagement, and multinational corporate exploitation. The same is true of Africans in England, the United States, and other nations where we face police violence, racial profiling and imprisonment, mis-education, physical and psychological torture, dysfunctional families and a capitalist imposed drug economy that criminalizes our people, especially the youth.

Sadly, this is not a new phenomenon. The origin of these dismal conditions of existence can be traced to the European Atlantic slave trade that began in earnest in the 16th century in the Americas. This infernal trafficking in human beings supplied skilled labor to the European colonies in north, central and South America for approximately 300 years. The unpaid, skilled labor demanded of enslaved Africans led to the amassing of tremendous wealth by European capitalist nations that were directly and indirectly involved in the slave trade and cash crop colonialism. The massive economic edifice called capitalism today was made possible by this primitive accumulation of wealth. The past five hundred years bear witness to the hyper exploitation of Africa and the inconceivable suffering of African people at the hands of the resulting capitalist, imperialist economy.

Like most problems that exist in Africa, inter-communal violence, that is, boundary and chieftaincy succession disputes, conflicts over land ownership, religious violence and "black-on-black crime", owes its origin to the parasitic relationship that exists between Africa and western imperialism. Quite often, we find ourselves engrossed in unreasonable disputes caused by disagreements concerning religion, tribalism and nationality. In most cases, people engage in violence and refuse to communicate with each other because they do not identify with the same religious group, tribe or ethnicity.

We must also acknowledge the outright terror orchestrated by capitalist forces that are desperately competing for control over our abundant natural resources. We must be clear, however, that despite their often violent competition, our imperialist enemies are never confused because they share a common interest: the exploitation of Africa's resources. In fact, Africa is being robbed everyday by Europe and the United States while we continue to have these meaningless disputes amongst ourselves. So, we must realize that inter-communal violence is but one of many consequences of centuries of colonial enslavement and capitalist exploitation that has robbed Africa of its resources and denied its people the right to enjoy peace and prosperity.

Truly speaking, I come from a place where the life span of an African has decreased to 37 years; a place where there is no electricity, no running water, no good roads, and no health facilities. In fact, a United Nations report says that three out of every five women who give birth in Sierra Leone are likely to die in labor. The country has the highest infant mortality rate in the world. Yet, Sierra Leone is rich in natural resources producing, for example, the world's most precious diamonds. There are about ninety multi-national corporations currently involved in the unjust exploitation of Sierra Leone's diamonds. One English corporation alone is taking out a hundred and twenty thousand carats from Sierra Leone every year with a single carat valued at US $60,000. The activities of these corporations have left thousands of our people homeless and landless, and completely isolated from their own natural resources.

So when we talk about violence and the causes of inter-communal violence in Africa, these are the issues we ought to examine. This is fundamentally important because we have to understand that the genocide and damage we suffer is still being perpetuated against us even as we gather here to discuss the question of reparations.

Imperialism works overtime to convince as many of us as possible that we are different. Likewise, it also works to persuade us that we are a part of the imperialist project. This is a fundamental contradiction that lays the basis for our understanding of the problems we collectively face as African people and what we have to do to change that situation.

Key to ending inter-communal violence in Africa is deepening our under-standing of our identity as one African people who are scattered and separated from each other as a consequence of imperialist aggression. We must understand that we are one people regardless of the fact that we may find ourselves isolated in Ghana, Nigeria, and the United States, England or some other place. We share a common history, a common identity and a common destiny. Knowing and appre-ciating who we are is critical to understanding the source of the contradictions we face today and what we must do to overturn our conditions as Africans.

In addition, we have to understand that reparations itself is equally part of our struggle for self-determination. And self-determination demands that we organize and commit ourselves to a revolutionary process designed to free us from neocolonialism and imperialism and take back our resources. So, addressing inter-communal violence demands that we build a revolutionary mass organiza-tion committed to organizing Africans around the world to identify and strug-gle against our oppressors. This will be tremendously significant in helping us strengthen our oneness as a people and our efforts to overcome our differences and overturn our difficulties.

This also brings us to the question of justice. By justice I mean a people's justice that is devoid of manipulation by imperialist forces and their cronies who work against the interest of the oppressed masses. I am pleased to tell you that we are currently involved in building an International Tribunal on Reparations for African People. This is a process that the Africanist Movement is currently participating in and it involves Africans from all around the African world. This Tribunal will be held in Berlin, Germany in June 2007 and will primarily serve as a tool for uniting all reparations movements and organizations around the world into a common effort that will enhance the significance of all our work and build the necessary practical global relationships and networks necessary for our success. Among other things, this tribunal will allow the international African community to achieve a communal explanation for the horrific material conditions that confront us. With this common knowledge, we can effectively address the impediments to our struggle whether it is inter-communal violence or some other issue resulting from our oppression by capitalism.

Discussions and planning meetings for this tribunal are ongoing. The first meeting was held in London, England, a second one was held in Paris last month. We are also meeting in Berlin as part of this process. We extend invitations to Africans around the world; it is an open and transparent process, and we are calling on all Africans to participate.

CHAPTER 6

INTERNAL CONFLICT OF THE AFRICAN LIBERATION MOVEMENT: THE AFRICAN SOCIALIST MOVEMENT VERSUS UHURU MOVEMENT

In 2005 the African Socialist Movement (then known as the Africanist Movement) invited representatives of the Uhuru Movement to participate in its first leadership conference held in Makeni, north of Sierra Leone. At the conference, relations between the African Socialist Movement (ASM) and Uhuru Movement were formalized. Both organizations agreed to join efforts to build an African Socialist International (ASI). This organization was to unite all African liberation organizations to build a common leadership for the unification and liberation of Africa. Relations between the African Socialist Movement (ASM) and the Uhuru Movement became engulfed with serious organizational and structural contradictions. This ultimately culminated into the break-up of the alliance. The Uhuru Movement, under the leadership of Omali Yeshitela, later published a slanderous article attacking the leadership of the African Socialist Movement (ASM) and its organization's efforts. The article was a calculated effort by Uhuru Movement members to destroy the reputation of the ASM and undermine its political work around the world. The publication itself came at a time when the African Socialist Movement, through its coalition with the National Democratic Alliance (NDA), was preparing to contest the general elections of 2012 in Sierra Leone. In fact, the article appeared a day after Chairman of the African Socialist Movement Chernoh Alpha M. Bah had arrived in Belgium as part of a national delegation observing the printing of voter identification cards by the Sierra Leone National Electoral Commission. The following article is a response to the Uhuru Movement's slanderous campaign. It gives a historical narrative of the relationship between the African Socialist Movement (ASM) and the Uhuru Movement. It highlights how leaders of the Uhuru Movement in Florida undermined the socialist efforts in Sierra Leone and West Africa. The article, first published by Africa News, was circulated in China and other parts of the world. It summarizes the betrayal of the African Socialist Movement (ASM) by the Uhuru Movement.

Omali Yeshitela and his Uhuru Movement have bombarded readers of the *Uhuru News* over the last couple of weeks with a clear and obvious calculated attempt to obsessively defame my hard-won reputation and the actual character of the African Socialist Movement (ASM) within the ranks of the African liberation movement.

It has been two weeks since the Uhuru Movement published an article containing fabricated and falsified information against me. Their intention was to isolate me and to equally destroy the sacrifices and great achievement of the thousands of young men and women in Sierra Leone. It was an attempt to tarnish the great efforts of individuals who have been struggling for the last eleven years to overturn the objective conditions of poverty and misery imposed upon their communities by imperialism and its neocolonial agents.

However, those with a knowledge of our relationship with the Uhuru Movement over the last few years will see right through the slander campaign and will be unsurprised at this cynical defamation of me and the ASM. Omali Yeshitela's group is once more trying to make victims out of people who have refused to submit themselves to the irrational dictatorship of the Uhuru Movement. In the article, Omali Yeshitela and his group had attempted to falsify history by dishonestly amputating the facts surrounding the chronology of events that governed our relationship with the Uhuru Movement.

What is more striking is the fact that the Uhuru Movement deliberately and unfairly attacked other individuals for standing in solidarity with the African Socialist Movement (ASM) and its leadership. Comrade Ajamu Bandele and his wife Iyapo Bandele, together with Matthew Willis, were unfairly attacked in the article. Omali Yeshitela wanted to smear the good reputation of people who express genuine support for the struggle of African people in Sierra Leone. This is a style of victimization and psychological violence unfairly employed by the Uhuru Movement against individuals who dissociate themselves from Omali Yeshitela's cultism.

I was obviously in Belgium when the Uhuru Movement first published its attack against me on the internet. I had initially decided not to respond to the article because I consider it to be a mere distraction from the very meaningful work that faces me. In fact, I sent Omali Yeshitela a correspondence after the article was published in which I told him that it is not my nature to respond to personal attacks directed against my work or disposition. I informed him that my reputation as an individual committed to the liberation of my people from the class contradictions of neocolonialism speaks for itself.

I am convinced that the fabricated allegations published against me by the Uhuru Movement lack the required credibility to destroy my impeccable history of consistent and committed struggle in West Africa. The simple reason is that the allegations of so-called "theft" and "criminality" imputed on me by Omali Yeshitela and his group had no validity. My humble credentials and profile as a combatant for the rights of African people to be free and self-determining supersede all the vile attack published by the Uhuru Movement. Again, the article achieved nothing outside the discharge of unprincipled diatribe against me and other members of the International Support Committee of the African Socialist Movement under the leadership of Comrade Ajamu Bandele.

So I initially paid no attention to the online debates between Uhuru Movement members and our supporters. Yet, after observing the very desperate attempt by the Uhuru Movement to falsify history through fabricated and distorted information around our relationship, I felt obliged to add my voice to the discussion. The objective of this article is to correct the inaccuracies and falsehood evident in the Uhuru Movement article. My response, therefore, is meant to put into correct historical perspective the actual relationship between the African Socialist Movement and Uhuru Movement, its background and accompanying contradictions.

Re-framing the context of the debate

The leadership of the African Socialist Movement (ASM) first initiated an open phone-call to the Uhuru Movement leader Omali Yeshitela a few days after they published their attack on the ASM and its leadership. The purpose of the phone-call by the ASM leadership was to demand a platform for an open public debate on the questions raised in the *Uhuru News* article. The African Socialist Movement was of the opinion that, since the Uhuru Movement had chosen to take its disagreement with the ASM leadership to the court of public opinion through its news website, they were obliged to allow an open discussion on the very website if they believed in the legitimacy of the allegations raised against the ASM leadership in the said article. Unfortunately, Omali Yeshitela could not accept the terms of an open public discourse on the contents of the article in question.

The Uhuru Movement had published an article unfairly, in which they attacked the characters and reputations of key revolutionaries within the African liberation movement, and they do not want to accommodate a response from the very individuals they slander. Their actions are not conditioned by correct revolutionary principles or the notion of natural justice (let both sides be heard).

A press release was issued by the ASM the following day, making this demand public and asking that pressure be placed on the leadership of the Uhuru Movement to allow the people whose names were mentioned in the article the right to respond to the allegations imputed on them. This was the only way the general masses that are ignorant of the basis of the contradictions between the ASM and Uhuru Movement would have an opportunity to arrive at sound conclusions. People must have access to the complete story by listening to both sides of the argument.

However, the Uhuru Movement did not accept these terms. In fact, we later learnt that the *Uhuru News*, for the first time since its creation in March 2006, adopted a policy of preventing people from making comments on any section of their website. They deliberately pursued their unprincipled enterprise of slander and character assassination. By so doing, they prevented ordinary people from having access to all the information relevant to the situation that created the actual controversy.

This article is therefore not a response to the Uhuru Movement but an opportunity for people who were denied the other side of the story by the Uhuru Movement to have access to truth that the Uhuru Movement is striving to obscure from the international African community. It is obvious that the article from the Uhuru Movement, which I am addressing in this essay, contains many windy and subjective narrations raising issues that are completely irrelevant and thoughtless. I will therefore concentrate only on those questions that appear to deal with the fabricated allegations. So in order to situate this discussion in its proper context, it will be fitting to examine the circumstances of the initial contact between the ASM and Uhuru Movement.

Our contact with the Uhuru Movement

Omali Yeshitela and his group have claimed that it was they who introduced me to the international community and to all the contacts I have in the African liberation movement.

That is to say, before our contact with the Uhuru Movement, we had no connections whatsoever outside of the borders of Sierra Leone, and that, by implication, I was unknown to the outside world. Through this premise, the Uhuru Movement assumed for itself that it was responsible for my political development, and by extension the formation of a revolutionary movement in Sierra Leone. This is not only wrong and incorrect but it also represents a complete distortion and falsification of history.

It was not Omali Yeshitela or the Uhuru Movement that started the struggle in Sierra Leone. Neither is Omali Yeshitela or anyone in the Uhuru Movement responsible for my entrance into revolutionary political life. More than that, it is not Omali Yeshitela or the Uhuru Movement that popularized me or the work of our Movement.

The fact is that I was born into a politically conscious family and by the age of twelve I was already actively involved in the political struggles of my country.

I need not state here the role I played during Sierra Leone's brutal civil conflict in the 1990s because it is well documented, and the Uhuru Movement is quite aware of that, even though they failed to mention it in their campaign of slander against me.

The truth is that for the last twenty or more years – since my childhood – I have been fighting for the emancipation of my people. I have committed my life and energy in defense of my people in times of war and periods of peace. I am both a victim and living witness of neocolonial oppression and exploitation. I grew-up in Sierra Leone at the apex of a war created by the ravenous exploitation of multinational corporations for control over the immense resources found in the country. I have lived through armed violence, survived it, and equally fought against it.

As a journalist for a number of years, I employed the tools of mass communication to articulate the concerns and interests of African workers and poor peasants displaced by imperialist sponsored wars in Liberia and Guinea. I have used my journalism in revolutionary terms to expose the oppression and exploitation of African communities. I need not trumpet the fact that my outstanding work and uncompromising stance against West Africa's neocolonial dictators during the 1990s forced me into exile and eventually landed me in some of the most oppressive prisons in the region.

It was this great sacrifice in defense of African people's right to self-determination that propelled me to a position of extreme danger and a platform of recognition within West Africa's political terrain. It was the desire to challenge this naked political oppression and economic exploitation that equally forced me to build many organizations throughout the period of my struggle. From organizing youths against military rule in Sierra Leone to organizing journalists to advocate for social transformation and end to oppression, I came across some of the most renowned activists in the region – from Liberia, Guinea and Nigeria to Ghana, Cameroon and beyond.

My organizing abilities have remained a subject of discussion from the ghettos of Kono, Eastern Sierra Leone in West Africa to the slums of Nairobi, Kenya in East Africa and the war-zones of Central Africa and refugee camps in Northern Africa. I have played host to many activists and fighters in Africa – from those in Casamance in Senegal to those in the Niger Delta in Nigeria and the Sudan People's Liberation Movement (SPLM) in South Sudan.

In 2001, I had organized one of the most populous militant revolutionary mass organizations in West Africa, which spread across the colonial borders of Sierra Leone to Guinea, right up to the Cameroons. In less than two years of its existence, the Africanist Movement mobilized a membership that was over seventy thousand youths across most parts of West Africa.

This organizational success was solely the result of astute leadership and dynamism that was unparalleled in contemporary times. All this success occurred at a time when we never knew of Omali Yeshitela and the Uhuru Movement.

Our first contact with the Uhuru Movement occurred sometime in June 2005 through an e-mail communication we received from Comrade Natalio Sowande Wheatley, a member of what was then called the London-chapter of the Uhuru Movement. Comrade Sowande, a PhD student at the time and from British Virgin Islands, had written to us informing us of a conference that was to be held in London to discuss efforts to build an organization referred to as the African Socialist International (ASI). Sowande's e-mail also requested our attendance to the conference and participation in the effort to build the ASI; a project of Omali Yeshitela. At the time, I was Director and leader of the Africanist Movement and simultaneously serving as a newspaper editor for one of Sierra Leone's leading newspapers in Freetown.

This e-mail correspondence from Comrade Sowande was discussed comprehensively in both leadership and mass meetings of the Africanist Movement, during which we resolved to explore a relationship with the Uhuru Movement as requested. The objective was to see how we would unite revolutionary movements across the African world into a single international organization. This was in line with the vision of the Africanist Movement.

In several correspondences with Comrade Sowande, we expressed our unambiguous unity to be part of any effort by African revolutionaries to unite our various struggles. It was in connection with such aspiration that we resolved to honor the invitation to meet with the leadership of the Uhuru Movement. As the leader of the Africanist Movement, it was my responsibility to proceed with the discussions as mandated by the members of my organization. This was how I travelled to London in October 2005 and met for the first time Omali Yeshitela and the few members forming the cabal of the Uhuru Movement. The costs associated with visas and travel to London for that meeting was paid by me and not the Uhuru Movement. It was at that October 2005 meeting in London that discussion around a possible relationship between the Africanist Movement and the Uhuru Movement was formally conducted. It was at that meeting also that a formal invitation was extended to the Uhuru Movement to attend the first leadership conference of the Africanist Movement, which was held in Makeni in November 2005, north of Sierra Leone.

The Uhuru Movement of Omali Yeshitela only entered in Sierra Leone in November 2005 as guests of the Africanist Movement to attend our leadership conference in Makeni. That conference was organized and financed by the resources of the Africanist Movement. All delegates of the Uhuru Movement, who included Gaida Kambon, Luwezi Kinshasa and Comrade Omavi Bailey, never paid for anything throughout the period of more than two weeks that they stayed in Sierra Leone as guests of the Africanist Movement.

It was during that conference that we first discovered tendencies of betrayal from the Uhuru Movement, when they secretly tried to recruit some members of the Africanist Movement into the Uhuru Movement or African People's Socialist Party. We even have a copy of an e-mail in our archives in which Gaida Kambon secretly reported to Omali Yeshitela that "the Africanist Movement is up for a grab." It was obvious from that point that the Uhuru Movement plotted to steal our membership. Evidences of these facts are equally well documented in a video footage put together by the Uhuru Movement from that conference.

Apart from distorting the narrative of the documentary, the Uhuru Movement produced a number of videos from footage of our activities that they sold throughout the world with no account made of the proceeds of the sales of such videos. Nobody knew how much money the Uhuru Movement generated for itself out of the fundraising activities they conducted in the name of "helping the struggle in Sierra Leone." Neither were they even honest enough to give a correct account of the chronology of events leading up to their connections with the Africanist Movement.

With all of these facts in mind, it is interesting that the Uhuru Movement attempted to create the impression that it was they who introduced me to the international world, and also that they want people to believe that it was Omali Yeshitela who is responsible for my political understanding and conclusion. This is completely wrong and dangerously misleading.

I had successfully built a revolutionary mass organization with hundreds of thousands of members across West Africa before the Uhuru Movement came in contact with me. In fact, the Uhuru Movement was undeniably attracted to my outstanding political work and proven organizational strength and capacity. Sadly, throughout the period of our relationship, they had always struggled to wrongfully ascribe to themselves the organizational capacity and strength of the Africanist Movement. They created the impression within the African community in the United States and United Kingdom that the genesis and actual existence of a revolutionary struggle in Sierra Leone and much of West Africa owes its credit to the Uhuru Movement. This was a completely misleading position. The Uhuru Movement was unknown in Sierra Leone before 2005, and it had never had a presence in Sierra Leone before then and still lacks an actual presence in Sierra Leone today.

Uhuru Movement tried to usurp our work

Since 2005, Omali Yeshitela and his group were anxiously scheming to subvert our work. They had created a false impression in the United States and England that they owned the Africanist Movement; that the existence and actual political development of our organization represented a practical manifestation of Omali Yeshitela's so-called leadership and "internationalism." This was a deliberate concoction by the Uhuru Movement to arrogantly place themselves above every organization in the African liberation movement. All propaganda materials from the Uhuru Movement falsely apportioned our work to the supposed success of Omali Yeshitela. This erroneous and misleading distortion that they put out into the world made them unwilling to accept an organizational relationship with the Africanist Movement where both organizations would function on equal terms. Our objective was to work with the Uhuru Movement in promoting the cause of African unity and liberation within a principled arrangement that was to ultimately result into the actual development of single, organic force on an international level. Omali Yeshitela wanted more than that: he preferred not only to lord over the Africanist Movement but embarked on a program to usurp our work.

Many of the comrades in Sierra Leone often complained about the misleading propaganda that was disseminated by the Uhuru Movement. The leadership of the Africanist Movement encouraged its members to accommodate the excesses with the understanding that we woud struggle with Omali Yeshitela and his group to realize the need to rectify such erratic conduct. This was to serve as the basis of continuous disagreement between us throughout the period.

The situation reached an alarming point when Diop Olugbala was sent by Omali Yeshitela to Sierra Leone in 2008 on the invitation of the Africanist Movement leadership. At the time, we had agreed with the Uhuru Movement on the need for a cross-exchange of training programs between our organizations. This was to allow members of both organizations to benefit from experiences outside of their own location. We knew that the Uhuru Movement had a lot to learn from our organizational techniques judging from our success in building a mass-based revolutionary movement. We were always concerned with the fact that the Uhuru Movement, with its multitude of organizations, lacked a mass presence and following even in St. Petersburg, Florida where it is headquartered.

Our hope was that the Uhuru Movement would learn how to build a mass organization if some of its organizers were to come to Sierra Leone and participate in the daily activities and programs of our movement. This was why we invited Diop Olugbala from the Uhuru Movement to Sierra Leone.

Unfortunately, we discovered from the welcome meeting we held for Diop Olugbala on the night of his arrival that he had been instructed by the Uhuru Movement leadership to come to Sierra Leone and recruit members of the Africanist Movement into the Uhuru Movement. In the process, Diop Olugbala immaturely incurred the wrath of members of the Africanist Movement. He offensively stated that his organization did not consider our movement a revolutionary organization. He said the only revolutionaries are those in the Uhuru Movement. This statement was completely outrageous and arrogant to the highest degree. It annoyed every single member of the Africanist Movement.

We sent a correspondence to Omali Yeshitela a few weeks later and expressed our dissatisfaction with the conduct of Diop Olugbala and the characterization of our movement. Omali Yeshitela distanced his organization from the utterances of Diop Olugbala and offered apologies for the disparaging remarks made by his representative. The Uhuru Movement realized that it was impossible for it to employ subterfuge to control the Africanist Movement.

Omali Yeshitela moves from subterfuge to co-optation

Having realized the futility of that strategy, Omali Yeshitela imagined that the best way to control the work of the Africanist Movement was by co-opting the leadership into the ranks of the Uhuru Movement. During a visit to the Uhuru House in Florida a month later, Omali Yeshitela asked me to take up membership of the Uhuru Movement. I stated emphatically that our position of unity with the Uhuru Movement was based on the objective of building the African Socialist International (ASI). I reminded them that this position is reflected in the 2005 communiqué passed at the leadership conference in Makeni announcing our unity to build the ASI.

The African Socialist International (ASI) was a skeletal project when the Uhuru Movement came in contact with us. It had no leadership structure and designations. It was its relationship with the Africanist Movement that gave oxygen to the ASI process and even the entire Uhuru Movement. The leadership of the Africanist Movement employed all the tools at its disposal to call on Africans across the world to be part of the process to build the ASI. It was our singular efforts at mobilization and mass propaganda that germinated the entire work of the ASI process, leading from a position of comatose to real life organizing. When we met the Uhuru Movement, the ASI was just a concept on paper with no structure and direction. Apart from the poorly attended yearly conferences, it achieved nothing absolute. It had no plan to galvanize actual organizational influence that would have ensured its presence on the continent.

The first real presence of the ASI in Africa was to occur with the advent of the Africanist Movement. Through the Africanist Movement and its mass presence, Omali Yeshitela egoistically posed as a "commander of the African revolution" even with his obvious incapability to build an actual organization. The Africanist Movement already had everything the Uhuru Movement had been dreaming of building for years. The first ever ASI conference with a real mass attendance to be held in the history of Omali Yeshitela's existence as a so-called revolutionary was the one conveyed by the Africanist Movement in Freetown, Sierra Leone during the month of October 2008. It was also under my leadership and directives that the ASI entered East Africa. Before then, there was never any presence of the Uhuru Movement or the ASI in any part of East Africa, either. None of this was stated by the Uhuru Movement in their desperate efforts to smear my reputation and character. The Uhuru Movement has never proved to us that they are capable of building an organization with a mass character. Omali Yeshitela's revolution and organizing capabilities have been limited only to the University Halls of North America and the poorly attended meetings of the Uhuru House in Florida and California.

The move to build a party

We knew of this extreme limitation of Omali Yeshitela and his Uhuru Movement. But we were determined to work with them to advance the effort to build a single international revolutionary organization of Africans across the world that would fight for the liberation and unification of African people. The draft constitution of the ASI provided that all organizations wishing to be part of the process should be known as the African People's Socialist Party (APSP) of the area in which they were established except in areas where for historical reasons this could not be possible. This provision within the ASI constitution was, in our view, designed to test the actual commitment of any organization wishing to be part of the process. Several discussions were held between August and September 2009 within the ranks of the Africanist Movement to determine how we could move into actualizing the communiqué passed at our leadership conference of 2005 in Makeni to build the ASI.

A segment of the regional leaders, fearing the treachery of the Uhuru Movement as reflected in the history of our relationship, refused to continue with efforts to build the ASI. They opted out of the Africanist Movement on grounds that they did not trust a relationship with the Uhuru Movement.

A final meeting was conveyed on October 5, 2009 to determine a way forward. At the meeting, attended by all regional leaders and organizers, more than eighty-five percent of the comrades resolved to follow the decision to transform the Africanist Movement into the African People's Socialist Party (APSP) of Sierra Leone. This was in line with the constitution of the ASI and its main resolution document. This was also in conjunction with the communiqué we passed at the 2005 leadership conference.

It was equally resolved at that very meeting that to avoid confrontation between those who had united with the idea to build the APSP of Sierra Leone and the few other comrades who objected to a further relationship with the Uhuru Movement; it was unanimously agreed by everyone that the Africanist Movement should be dissolved. A communiqué announcing our decision to dissolve the Africanist Movement to build the APSP was issued on October 8, 2009 and circulated widely across the world. The *Uhuru News* published the said communiqué with enthusiasm.

Omali Yeshitela's lack of sincerity destroyed our efforts

Our experiment to build the APSP suffered a major setback due to the lack of sincerity by Omali Yeshitela to genuinely build a real revolutionary party that would actually contest for real power. The Uhuru Movement, in its slanderous article, stated wrongly that the decision to dissolve the Africanist Movement was unilaterally done and that the consultative conference held at the British Council Hall in Freetown was a fait accompli to position myself within the ranks of the petty bourgeoisie in Sierra Leone. They even erroneously stated that I actually flouted the laws of Sierra Leone by announcing the formation of a party without having it registered.

This is completely dishonest. What the Uhuru Movement failed to state was the fact that the decision to form the APSP of Sierra Leone was the direct instructions of Omali Yeshitela. The entire leadership of the Uhuru Movement was aware of the limitations imposed on our struggle by the repugnant neocolonial legislations in force in Sierra Leone.

We have copies of several correspondences with Omali Yeshitela on this question. The Uhuru Movement wanted us to establish a branch in Sierra Leone but they were unwilling to accept the burden of organizing such a formation in the country. At the said consultative conference to build the APSP, which had come about as a consequence of severe deliberation from our movement forces, they made a last unsuccessful attempt to enlist conference participants into their organization. They could not accomplish this sinister objective; they blamed me for preventing them from recruiting members of our organization into the Uhuru Movement. It became obvious that what the Uhuru Movement was interested in was subverting the work of our movement in a bid to create a branch under their leadership and control in Sierra Leone.

Our actual disagreement with Uhuru Movement

Our actual disagreement with the Uhuru Movement ultimately reached its climax in January 2010, a month after the transformation of the Africanist Movement into the APSP of Sierra Leone. The Sierra Leone government of Ernest Bai Koroma had introduced a 15% tax increase on goods and services across the country at a time when workers' salaries had remained abysmally low.

A press conference was convened in the name of the newly established APSP in which we called for a struggle against the new tax legislation. The following day, shops and businesses across the country remained closed. That evening, the IMF and World Bank representatives issued a joint statement calling on the people of Sierra Leone to support the new tax legislation. This position also warranted us to issue another statement condemning the World Bank and IMF officials. The following day, the country's Political Parties Registration Commission (PPRC) issued an ultimate ban on the existence of the APSP on technical grounds that it was not a registered political party in the country. I organized several media events to challenge the position of the PPRC but it was obvious that for the APSP to exist in Sierra Leone, it had to fulfill the conditions laid down by the laws of the country. To become a registered party, the APSP would need to maintain four offices across the country and to pay a registration fee of US$500. There were no such offices for the APSP's operation, neither was there any money available to pay the stipulated registration fees.

We appeared to be faced with a dilemma. We were no longer allowed to organize in the name of the APSP of Sierra Leone. We attempted several discussions with the leadership of the Uhuru Movement on a way forward. Omali Yeshitela's interest was not to legitimize the APSP; he requested that the idea of the party should be abandoned. He wanted a branch of his International People's Democratic Uhuru Movement (InPDUM) to be established in Sierra Leone in place of the APSP.

It became obvious that what the Uhuru Movement wanted was to justify that they had a branch in Sierra Leone and nothing more. They were never committed to building an actual revolutionary party that would struggle for the conquest of real political power. We refused to form InPDUM. We told Omali Yeshitela that we were not a branch of his group. We believed that the formation of InPDUM in Sierra Leone was in direct conflict with the process to build the African Socialist International (ASI). The ASI was the actual basis of our relationship with the Uhuru Movement. We communicated our position to Omali Yeshitela and the entire leadership of the Uhuru Movement. The Uhuru Movement was very annoyed with our position not to build a branch of Omali Yeshitela's group in Sierra Leone.

They later resolved on a strategy of poaching the less developed members of our organization. They contacted members who were mainly part of the security department of our organization into accepting bribes and promises of travel to the United States for further political training with the Uhuru Movement. Some of these individuals were part of the group of security forces we had assigned as close protection guards to Omali Yeshitela during his visit to Sierra Leone for the consultative conference of November 2009.

Reports of several phone calls and e-mail correspondences from Uhuru Movement leaders to some of our members were communicated to the leadership of our Movement. We realized that the Uhuru Movement had embarked on a program of subversive activities against our leadership on the ground in a bid to divide and conquer our base.

Uhuru Movement uses AAPDEP to divide our base

This program of subversion became more obvious when a woman we had sent to the United States for medical training and fundraising with the Uhuru Movement was appointed by Omali Yeshitela to establish a branch of his organization in Sierra Leone. The woman was a nurse midwife we recruited to help kick-start a community healthcare program that would tackle the high incidences of infant and maternal mortality in Sierra Leone. She was instructed by the Uhuru Movement to establish a branch of the All-African People's Development and Empowerment Project (AAPDEP) in Sierra Leone.

The woman saw the Uhuru Movement's offer as a golden opportunity to earn a living. The Uhuru Movement worked out a monthly salary for her to enable it control of her actions and activities. She also gave the Uhuru Movement the impression that she leads a women's movement in Sierra Leone called Women in National Development (WIND), made up of traditional birth attendants.

The so-called WIND organization did not exist. But for the Uhuru Movement, they saw what they were looking for. They wanted someone they could readily use as a "poster-child" to defend the myth of their existence in West Africa. They had given this impression to the African community in the United States and elsewhere. They couldn't afford to have that myth broken down by obvious reality.

Uhuru Strategy ends up in opportunist triangle

When she returned to Sierra Leone, the nurse midwife hurriedly put together the semblance of an organization to actualize what she told the Uhuru Movement. She entered into a relationship with the Passengers Welfare Organization (PAWEL), a group that was running the facade of a Nursing School in Sierra Leone without any legal status. The leader of the group was desperately looking out for financial support to capacitate his nursing school. Most people trained by the school were not admitted into mainstream nursing practice. This debilitated the organization and its leadership.

In 2007, a friend of our movement had introduced the leader of this organization to us. We were working on a program of expansion that aimed at building a mass-based coalition of organizations. Our objective was to deepen our mass influence in the country in order to advance a struggle for national democratic rights. PAWEL was one of forty organizations that we enlisted as part of this broader coalition.

In August 2007, the Passengers Welfare Organization worked with us to coordinate the visit of representatives of the Sudan People's Liberation Movement (SPLM). The SPLM had come to Sierra Leone to seek the support of our movement for the Sudan Sensitization Project (SSP). The SSP was designed to win worldwide support for the independence of South Sudan. We never continued any relationship with PAWEL after the SPLM program. After the elections of

2007, the leadership of PAWEL visited President Ernest Bai Koroma, who had recently come to power, to pledge their support for his government.

It was this organization that the Uhuru Movement nurse midwife in Sierra Leone entered into a relationship with. PAWEL leaders were promised that the Uhuru Movement was going to fund its Nursing School if they were to transform the name of the school into AAPDEP. The Nursing School of PAWEL was transformed into the so-called AAPDEP Nursing School. The Uhuru Movement posted pictures of students from the school and falsely claimed that they were being trained as nurses by the help of the Uhuru Movement.

In January 2012, members of the Uhuru Movement visited Sierra Leone on the invitation of the nurse midwife. The visit coincided with a graduation of students from the school. Members of the community whose relations were students of the school attended the event.

The Uhuru Movement delegation took pictures and video footage of the event and of the school and the students. Returning to the United States, they hurriedly published these pictures as evidence of their work in Sierra Leone. They were desperate to show that they had a presence in the country.

On the side of the nurse midwife and the leaders of PAWEL, it gave them some confidence in that they were able to pull together a crowd of people to present for the cameras of the Uhuru Movement representatives. They assumed this would allow them to extort funds from unsuspecting North Americans in the United States under the guise of reparations and solidarity.

A triangle of opportunism developed with Uhuru Movement on the one side, the nurse midwife on the other, and the PAWEL leadership in the middle. We looked at this comic work with amusement.

The Uhuru Movement, which claims to be a revolutionary party, was now actually working with the most opportunistic forces in Sierra Leone. We knew that the comic enterprise was to help Omali Yeshitela defend the myth of his organization's presence in Sierra Leone. His strategy was to use AAPDEP to seduce poor Africans who were told that projects and jobs would be provided to them if they were to join his organization.

It was through this method that the Uhuru Movement went on to adopt existing kindergarten schools in rural communities in the south of Sierra Leone. These schools are actually run by church organizations and community partnership boards. The Uhuru Movement, through its opportunistic allies, took photographs of these schools to mislead its audience of white supporters in North America. These unsuspecting North Americans were regularly extorted by Uhuru Movement members in the name of contributing to the work in Africa.

What these white supporters of Omali Yeshitela have not realized is that the Uhuru Movement was not implementing programs in Africa with AAPDEP. This was a complete farce. There was no single work that was done by the nurse midwife or any of its associates in Sierra Leone that is tied to any revolutionary work or effort. The projects that Omali Yeshitela claimed to have established in Sierra Leone had been there before the Uhuru Movement came into the country. Most of these institutions are non-political formations funded by local or international non-governmental organizations (NGOs). To some of these organizations, Yeshitela's group is nothing but an NGO that they expect to get funds from.

Where then is the Uhuru Movement in all of this? This is the greatest puzzle that the Uhuru Movement members have been struggling to solve. They think the solution lies in smearing my reputation and demonizing the ASM. The fact is that Omali Yeshitela and his Uhuru Movement have found themselves in a complete dilemma they do not know how to get out of.

It is however important for people to understand that the Uhuru Movement has no organizational presence in Sierra Leone. The few individuals they rely on to build InPDUM have neither organizational skills nor experience to pull together anything meaningful for the Uhuru Movement. They are individuals accustomed to grant-seeking type work. They have no knowledge of revolutionary work. The Uhuru Movement knows this is exactly the case.

This is why I conclude that Omali Yeshitela has no moral authority to question the correctness or incorrectness of our tactics and strategy. The effectiveness of the Uhuru Movement and Omali Yeshitela, in my view, will only be measured and tested when they are able to build a real revolutionary organization with a mass character. Until they are able to accomplish this, whatever they pretend on doing amounts to childish gibberish. My position on this and other questions relative to the Uhuru Movement and Omali Yeshitela are directly informed by a scientific assessment of their work and conduct during the few years of our operation with them.

The African Socialist Movement (ASM) under my leadership will continue to fight for the liberation of our people and will never succumb to any effort by any organization or individual to destroy our vision and great sacrifices.

CHAPTER 7

UNITY OF THE AFRICAN LIBERATION MOVEMENT: A PREREQUISITE FOR LIBERATION

The following is an excerpt from a speech delivered by Chernoh Alpha M. Bah at the opening ceremony of the West Africa regional conference of socialists and progressives organized by the Africanist Movement at the Miatta Conference Centre in Freetown, Sierra Leone from October 20-22, 2008

I am extremely humbled today by the onus of presenting the opening address at the first West Africa regional conference of African Socialists and progressives taking place in Freetown. While it may sound irrelevant for me to reiterate the significance of our gathering here today, I believe there is no doubt in our minds that history is in the making once again in Africa.

The late Kwame Nkrumah organized the first conference of independent African states fifty years ago in Accra, Ghana. At the time, much of Africa was still under direct colonial domination, so very few of the independent states of Africa were present. The 1958 Accra conference re-invigorated the desperate desires of African people for freedom from colonial domination. It remains one of Nkrumah's greatest contributions towards the total liberation of Africa and the unification of the continent under an all-African socialist government.

In the fifty years since that historic conference, several initiatives have occurred at the national, regional and international levels to unify Africa and liberate our people from the depredations of imperialism and capitalism. Many suggest that the establishment of the Organization of African Unity (OAU) at the 1963 Addis Ababa conference represented the climax of such efforts began during the 1950s and 1960s. We cannot over emphasize the fact that the OAU, the organization that preceded the African Union, has not lived up to Nkrumah's vision for continental unity and the total liberation of Africa from imperialist domination.

The current attempts by heads of "micro" states in Africa as reflected in the activities of the African Union cannot unite the continent politically and economically. The total liberation and unification of Africa must be directed from below by the African masses. Only an organization led by workers in alliance with the peasants can successfully bring about revolutionary change and unification under an all-African socialist government.

This task requires a correct theoretical and ideological understanding that is rooted in a scientific analysis of our conditions of existence at all levels of development. A sad thing that has occurred following the defeat of the African liberation movement in Africa and other places by the end of the 1960s is the notion that the struggle was over. The murder of Patrice Lumumba in Congo, the overthrow of Nkrumah in Ghana, the assassination of Amilcar Cabral of Guinea Bissau, the murder of Malcolm X and the defeat of the Black Panther Party in the United States, robbed African people of authentic leadership, leaving us at the mercy of imperialism and the exploitative tendencies of capitalism. This defeat has reinforced the notion that Africa is now "independent" and that Africans possess self-determination. It was like history was complete and there was no reason or point for continued struggle.

The ensuing years of "independence", that is, the 1950s through the 1970s, have witnessed very little improvement in the unbearable living conditions of the people. Today, "postcolonial" realities in Africa severely compromise the people's ability to exercise self-determination. Some of our people are even arguing that we were better under colonialism than we are now. If this is the case we have to ask ourselves the following questions: What was wrong with the anti-colonial movement and the struggle of the 1960s? Why is it that with fifty years of "independence", Africa still faces some of the most devastating challenges and problems in the world? What is responsible for the numerous socio-economic and political contradictions that continue to threaten peace, growth and development on the continent? And why has continental unity become an illusion; a seemingly impossible task to accomplish?

These are among the many questions that the first West Africa regional conference of socialists and progressives seeks to answer. Providing answers to these questions will give us an understanding of the historical circumstances of our own existence and what is responsible for the innumerable problems confronting us. It will at the same time inform us of our collective responsibility as a people to overcome these conditions and establish a future for our children and generations yet unborn.

We Africans are a determined people and we will continue to struggle on every front to affect meaningful and productive change in the conditions that are forced upon us by imperialism and neocolonialism. While there exists genuine forces and groups on the continent and beyond, committed to the complete liberation of the masses, it is obvious that the absence of an international revolutionary movement of African workers has seriously affected our capacity to organize and handle a holistic revolutionary program at all levels of struggle. This imposes serious constraints on most movements and individuals sincerely struggling to regain control of our resources and ultimately facilitate the unification of Africa. This limitation has manifested itself in different forms including limited resources, inadequate political education, limited training, ill-equipped revolutionary ventures and general inexperience and limited exposure to theory and discourse among African revolutionaries. This is the most significant gap that this conference sets to address.

It is significant for us to note that this conference is occurring at a crucial moment in history, a period when the entire capitalist economy is faced with tremendous crisis and great uncertainties about its ability to survive. It is pertinent for us to understand that the ongoing crisis of imperialism and the collapse of the global capitalist economy have been brought about, in part, by the rising resistance of the oppressed masses of the world who are determined to break free from the parasitic chains of capitalism. All around the world, from Latin America to Asia to the Middle East and the Pacific, capitalism is being challenged by the struggles of the oppressed masses. We are faced with a defining moment in history; a moment that demands from us our collective efforts and contributions to further deepen this crisis of imperialism and accelerate the death of capitalism. Africa must not assume a passive role in this world historical process. It must be understood that the fight for socialism is a genuine struggle for popular democracy and the creation of a new world in the hands of the workers and poor peasants. Africa must move to the position of once again becoming the subject of history rather than an object of history. This is the opportunity that we present with this conference.

Our task today is to unite and consolidate our efforts into an international organization capable of developing the tactics and strategies necessary to deepen the current crisis of capitalism and forward the uncompromising liberation and unification of Africa and African people around the world. African revolutionaries, progressives and individuals committed to the struggle for African unity and liberation must launch discussions geared towards adopting the international strategy and approach that this period presents to us. Taking our struggles out of isolation should be part of the guiding philosophy and principle for the actualization of the vision for a free, united socialist Africa. It is my hope that by the end of this conference we will have concrete recommendations to forward the uncompromising liberation and unification of Africa and African people around the world. We must adopt a comprehensive Plan of Action for building and consolidating our movement around the world. This West Africa conference is part of a series of meetings scheduled between now and next year in all the regions of the continent to pull together forces that will participate in the work to build and consolidate our movement. It is our hope that those of you present here today will find time to participate in this process.

At this juncture, let me express my profound appreciation to all of you for attending this historically significant event and for being a part of the process to liberate and unite our people and our Africa. Let me also congratulate the Comrades in the Africanist Movement for taking upon the arduous task of hosting this huge conference. This is surely a victory against our detractors and enemies of the revolution. It is a major step towards the realization of our objective. My strength and determination to struggle has always been made possible through the unshaken courage, zeal and commitments of all of you to the total liberation and unification of our people. Let us build on these enviable qualities and continue to work assiduously for the future of our people. It is surely a difficult task we have set for ourselves but there is nothing more pleasurable to do than the work to create a better future for generations yet unborn. Victory is ours and we will surely win!

PART III
MULTINATIONAL CORPORATIONS, ELECTIONS & RESOURCE EXPLOITATION IN WEST AFRICA

CHAPTER 8
GUINEA: GENERAL LANSANA CONTE AND THE WESTERN CORPORATE MAFIA

In 1984, following the death of anti-colonial leader Ahmed Sekou Toure, former presidential guard General Lansana Conte came to power in a coup that overthrew the Democratic Party of Guinea (PDG) and its socialist program. Ten years after the coup, the military dictatorship installed by Conte and his cohorts had transformed the once emerging socialist country into a hub of neo-liberalism. Hundreds of multinational companies, mainly from North America, occupy the country and are actively engaged in resource exploitation and expropriation. In this article, Chernoh Alpha M. Bah reviews the political and economic situation of Guinea since General Conte assumed power. He concludes that the country is now a perfect example of the failure of neo-liberalism on the continent of Africa. Bah also provides an analysis of the country within the context of France's geo-political machinations in West Africa. This article was first published in June 2006 in the Africanist Bulletin and later appeared in several publications around the world.

President Lansana Conte of Guinea celebrates his 71st birthday this year. Twenty-two years have passed since he came to power in 1984 in a coup following the death of Ahmed Sekou Toure. Conte's power grab ended the Toure regime's on-going struggle against French imperialism. Anti-colonial resistance waged by Africans and other colonized people grew significantly following the end of the second imperialist war. France, like all other imperialist nations, found it impossible to contain the people's struggle for self-determination. Sekou Toure's leading role in the people's struggle against colonial domination in West Africa became a major factor that French imperialism had to contend with during the late 1950s and 60s. Toure stood firmly against Charles de Gaulle's 1958 referendum that aimed at transforming "French West Africa" into nominal independent states whose economies and politics would be under direct French control. It is easy to understand Toure's anti-neocolonial position. France, like other imperialist nations, had enjoyed tremendous economic benefits from its colonies, leaving the African masses poor and destitute. France also owed a great debt to African soldiers who fought in Europe during the second imperialist war. They played a key role in reinstating the De Gaulle regime following its forced expulsion from France by the Germans.

Enforced by a colonial detachment stationed in Dakar, Senegal since 1800, French colonial policy in West Africa divided the Africans into subjects and citizens. For example, Africans in the "communes" in Senegal were considered French citizens, enjoying some "privileges" as opposed to Africans in areas like Guinea-Conakry, Mali, Burkina Faso, Ivory Coast and the rest of the territories under direct French colonial rule. This policy of division and exclusion facilitated the extraction of resources from the partitioned African states and deterred the development of any organizations seeking to overthrow the colonial administration. Consequently, the "African elites" in Dakar and the other communes in Senegal considered themselves French citizens and refused to unite with the anti-colonial aspirations of the suffering African masses in other areas. Most of them, including Blaize Diagne , saw the struggle to overthrow French colonialism as a direct threat to the positions they held in the colonial administration in Paris.

De Gaulle proposed that the African territories under direct French rule should vote to become members of a "French Community of nations" that would allow France undeniable access to the economy and resources of Africa with France supposedly undertaking "economic development" in the said territories. Sekou Toure was the only African leader in "French West Africa" to vote against the proposal, arguing that he preferred to be poor in liberty than to be wealthy in slavery. Toure's resistance forced France to withdraw from Guinea. So great was France's displeasure that, upon their departure, they stripped their administrative offices in Conakry bare, even removing office furniture and telephone wiring.

Sekou Toure was then faced with the challenge of maintaining the independence and unity of the African masses in Guinea against imperialist machinations to discredit and overthrow his administration. A Portuguese-led attempt to overthrow his government in 1970 failed, succeeding only in deepening the people's unity against imperialism. Toure attempted to adopt a socialist system in an effort to build the economy of Guinea and unite the people in the struggle against the forces of imperialism that were working to overthrow him. Lansana Conte's forced ascension to power ended Toure's attempt to deepen and broaden the struggle. France and the United States described his taking office as "the beginning of a new era in the history of Guinea." Despite the fact that Conte worked under Sekou Toure as an army general, he was determined to undermine Toure's efforts.

Indeed, Guinea under Conte represented "a new era" that changed the course of the people's struggle against imperialism. Since 1984, Conte has worked for the interest of France, the United States and the various imperialist nations who currently control the economy and have absolute access to all the resources in Guinea. In 1993, Conte successfully transformed himself into a civilian president through an electoral process organized and staged-managed by the United States and France. To maintain their neocolonial puppet in power, the United States and France developed a military and security apparatus, trained and equipped, to suppress the people's struggle for freedom. Like all the successive governments that emerged in Africa after the 1960s, Conte's administration and his two decades of governance have represented misery, poverty, oppression and deprivation to the people.

The imperialist exploitation of Guinea has increased since the death of Sekou Toure. Their primary motivating factor is their desire to control the mineral and other resources of the country. Guinea has one of the world's largest deposits of bauxite, a fine white metallic powder refined into alumina and smelted to become aluminum. The country contains one third of the world's recoverable bauxite reserves, which has remained Guinea's main export and largest source of foreign exchange. Guinea's bauxite and iron mines, once controlled by the African masses, are now owned and operated by three of the world's largest aluminum companies - Alcoa in the United States, Alcan of Canada and Rusal of Russia.

Like in most parts of Africa, the mad-rush for control of the continent's resources has even led to a contest between the imperialist nations themselves. For instance, Global Alumina Production Corporation (GAPCO), a Japanese company partially owned by industrial conglomerates Marubeni and Mitsubishi, signed a definitive agreement in October 2004 with the government of Guinea to build a US$2 billion alumina refinery in the northwestern mining town of Sangaredi. The agreement gives Japan absolute control over the biggest bauxite-mining complex in the world, thereby infringing upon the strategic interests of US corporate interests in Guinea. This Japanese venture was described as the largest mineral project undertaken in West Africa, until last year when a consortium of international oil companies led by Exon Mobil opened up a US$3.7 billion project to develop the oilfields of southern Chad that allowed the extraction of oil via a pipeline to the coast of Cameroon.

From 2004, the United States struggled in vain to get Lansana Conte to cancel the agreement signed with GAPCO. From the U.S. perspective, the 2.8 million tons of ore that GAPCO extracts every year was bad enough, but the fact that the agreement also provided for the construction of a refinery to convert the ore to alumina had seriously strained relations. The Japanese intrusion directly affected Global Alumina Corporation (GAC), a US company that uses the vast bauxite resources of Guinea to produce alumina for sale to the global aluminum industry.

GAC has its headquarters in New York and administrative offices in London, Montreal and Conakry.

Ironically, Conte's insatiable desires have entangled the nation's resources in the scramble of the various western nations to control the country's resources, placing him in direct confrontation with the United States and France. Since 2004, France and US backed protests by opposition parties headed by western-trained elites to bring down Conte and restore their interests in Guinea. They persuaded the European Union and other so-called western "donor countries" to cut-off "all aid" to the government of Guinea. Prof. Alpha Conde , a former lecturer at Sorbonne University in Paris, together with Ba Mamadou, a former World Bank Consultant, and Sidya Toure, a former IMF employee, have formed an opposition coalition supported and backed by both France and the United States to challenge the government of Conte. The opposition coalition's only hope of success was to manipulate the plight of the suffering African masses in Guinea and exploit their conditions to their own advantage. This has proven to be, however, an illusion, a fruitless strategy because none of the so-called opposition coalition leaders want to step-down and submit to a single leader.

Aware that France and the United States want to remove him from power, Conte amended the constitution in order to remain president for life. Suffering from ill health and a failed neocolonial bureaucracy, Conte continues to work to transform the state into a "royal possession" to be controlled by his family after his death. The security apparatus is used by Conte to suppress the urgency and determination of the African masses in Guinea to defeat imperialism. But with the people's growing determination for change, his reliance on the military and police to secure him is becoming shaky.

In 2005, a coup attempt staged by some junior officers left him nearly dead. In response, Conte sacked some 2,000 soldiers, including the head of the Guinean armed forces, General Mamadou Bailo Diallo. In December of 2005, 1,872 military personnel, including four colonels, 10 lieutenant-colonels, 39 majors, 93 captains and 1,727 non-commissioned officers were dismissed from the army based on Conte's fears that they might overthrow his government. With an army whose loyalty was increasingly unstable, Conte's continued presence in Guinea's political scene was extremely doubtful. A trade union strike over low wages and deplorable conditions of service nearly brought down the government. Unfortunately, the trade unions lacked the vision and ability to transform the conditions of the suffering masses in Guinea by overturning the neocolonial system.

CHAPTER 9

GUINEA: HOW AMERICAN CORPORATE INTERESTS CREATED A NEOCOLONIAL REGIME

In January and February 2007, hundreds of thousands of young people in Conakry and several other cities in the provincial parts of Guinea rose up in mass protests against the regime of General Lansana Conte calling for his removal from power. Conte came to power in 1984 following a military coup that overthrew Ahmed Sekou Toure's Democratic Party of Guinea (PDG) and its socialist program. Conte's coup occurred a month following the death of Ahmed Sekou Toure himself. He was to rule the country as a military leader for ten years before holding elections that transformed him into a civilian president up to his death in December 2008. His government was characterized by political repression, police brutality, corruption and suppression of civil liberties. The worsening economic situation caused mainly by state corruption and organized exploitation of the mineral wealth of the country created discontent among the masses, most of whom suffer from massive unemployment. Faced with turmoil in the region due to rebel wars in neighboring Liberia and Sierra Leone and growing agitation for economic and political reforms from the people, Conte's regime became aggressively brutal and violent. Police brutality against ordinary people, mainly jobless youths, became rampant across the country. This was to culminate into open spontaneous battles between the people and the anti-riot police and paramilitary troops. By 2003, due to ill-health and a corrupt political bureaucracy, Conte was no longer in control of the country's affairs. Protests were a daily occurrence in Conakry and other places. In 2005, a failed coup plot by the army to remove him from power resulted into serious purges within the military. In 2007, following escalation of commodity prices, hundreds of thousands of youths took to the streets in Conakry and other major cities across the country calling for the removal of Lansana Conte. The two months of protests led trade union leaders and civil society organizations to broker a deal with the Conte regime that allowed for the appointment of a new Prime Minister, Lansana Kouyate, to run the affairs of the government. Positions formerly held by Lansana Kouyate, the new Prime Minister, include executive secretary of the Economic Community of West African States (ECOWAS) and the United States Agency for International Development (USAID). The African Socialist Movement (then known as the Africanist Movement), one of the organizations that engineered protests against the Conte regime, was dissatisfied with the compromise. In the following article, which first appeared on the Africanist Bulletin and was later published by several newspapers across the world in 2007, Chernoh Alpha M. Bah summarizes the reasons for the Movement's protest against Lansana Kouyate's appointment, exposing that it represents a political compromise that secures the interests of American multinational interests and their neo-colonial project in Guinea. The article directly accuses the United States of the manipulation.

Guinea's new Prime Minister, Lansana Kouyate has announced his plans to organize what he describes as transparent elections in December 2007. This public announcement follows Kouyate's recent visit to Washington where he met with U.S Secretary of State Condoleezza Rice as well as senior officials of the World Bank and International Monetary Fund to discuss an elections agenda for Guinea and military support from the United States to his government.

In a recent interview with *All Africa Global Media*, Kouyate reported that his meeting with Condoleezza Rice was productive because the United States made commitments to support his government.

"We have so many challenges. The issue of security is paramount…the administration in the countryside is non-existent because the infrastructure – police stations, prison, and prefecture – was destroyed during the turmoil. But I have received total commitment from Rice that the US is going to back the process and we are working out how to reinforce the Guinean army, how to reinforce our police, our security system, and how to help us hold transparent elections in December 2007," Kouyate told the *All Africa Media Group* in Washington few days ago.

The Africanist Movement (AM) views Kouyate as a puppet imposed upon the masses of African people to facilitate the theft of the vast aluminum resources in Guinea by the United States and its corporate allies.

The Africanist Movement's position on Kouyate is informed by historical evidence, not merely from an assessment of his current political role in Guinea. Kouyate worked as a United States political agent several years ago. Prior to becoming the executive secretary of the Economic Community of West African States (ECOWAS), Kouyate worked with the United States Agency for International Development (USAID), then the United Nations and later served as a special envoy of France in Ivory Coast. A clear understanding of Kouyate's current role and function in Guinea can best be obtained from a study of the controversial circumstances that led to his appointment, described by the petty bourgeoisie as a "consensus prime minister."

Kouyate's appointment to prime minister is not the product of popular support neither is it the true outcome of the mass uprisings in January and February against the Conte regime. It is, rather, the consequence of the illogical, insincere and dishonest decisions of Guinea's trade union leadership and certain sections of the civil society movement who themselves are working, as agents of US imperialism and its corporate allies, Alcoa and Alcan, to carry out a sponsored program for regime change. These leading North American corporations increased their penetration of Guinea's mining sector in the years following the death of Ahmed Sekou Toure and the appointment of General Lansana Conte, and they remain the dominant corporations controlling and exploiting aluminum and iron ore from Guinea notwithstanding the continued presence of the Russian Aluminum Company (Rusal).

By 2006, for instance, Alcoa alone - the world's leading producer and manager of primary aluminum – is believed to have extracted 86,300 tons of bauxite daily from its mining concessions in Guinea from which 9,575 tons of aluminum was smelted and 8,810 tons of aluminum products were produced, including consumer brands like Reynolds Wrap, Alcoa wheels and Baco household wraps.

For a very long time, however, this North American corporate monopoly over the bauxite and iron ore reserves in Guinea went unchallenged. The Lansana Conte regime, which came to power in a 1984 coup sponsored by France and the United States against the then socialist government of Ahmed Sekou Toure, depended on the capital provided by these imperialist corporations to support his administration. The aim was to ensure that the Conte regime maintains a free enterprise economy that guarantees their hyper-exploitation of Guinea's mineral wealth.

Due to persuasion from the United States and France, Conte consequently drafted a new mining policy for Guinea in 1986, just two years after he assumed power. The policy, known as the 1986 Mining Code, based largely on French law, gave away the mining sector of the economy to western capitalist corporations. It provided a range of guarantees and tax incentives for the development of mining capital by western capitalist corporations allowing them ownership of at least 85% of any mining venture in Guinea.

The code also established a new department, the Centre for Mining Promotion and Development (CPDM), which was financed by the World Bank and International Monetary Fund. This enabled the Conte regime to conduct joint surveys with several capitalist mining corporations, which resulted in the identification of strategic mineral deposits in several parts of the country, including the richest bauxite reserves at Sangaredi and Kerouani in the far east of Guinea and the creation of a national database of geological information.

Through this program, at least a hundred multinational corporations, some of which were subsidiaries of both Alcoa and Alcan, gained unfettered access and control over Guinea's mineral wealth between 1986-2005. Guinea's Ministry of Mines and Geological Surveys in its 2005 Mining Sector Report revealed that about 100 multinational corporations are actively mining across the country. These did not include corporations owned by dubious individual magnates involved in nefarious activities around the world or corporations operating under the pseudo-ownership of some senior corrupt officials of the Conte regime.

The United States and France helped Conte to develop a military and security infrastructure to protect the regime and facilitate the theft and transfer of Guinea's natural resources by the various multinational corporations operating in the country. Since assuming power in 1984, opposition to Conte's policies has been suppressed. A political mafia has emerged that exploits the masses and thrives on mismanagement of resources, embezzlement of public funds, political abuse, rogue alliances and corrupt contracts with western capitalist corporations.

To enforce the dictates of US imperialism and its allies, the Conte regime used the military and the police against organized opposition to his government. In 1993, Conte won a controversial election organized and rigged by France and the United States on his behalf to legitimize his rogue regime. Since then, all subsequent elections have been rigged by Conte's Party of Unity and Progress (PUP).

But throughout the period, the United States and France committed themselves to supporting the Conte regime only because he upheld the interests of the leading North American corporations operating in Guinea. In its 2005 Annual Report on Guinea, for example, the United States Agency for International Development (USAID) stated that: "the United States strategic interest in Guinea is to promote increased US private investment in Guinea's emerging economy as there are several large US Corporations in Guinea possessing significant shares of their respective markets."

What this implies is that the United States was prepared to go to any length to secure and increase its corporate exploitation of and monopoly over Guinea's vast aluminum and other strategic resources. This was in fact a key factor in Washington's support for the Liberians United for Reconciliation and Democracy (LURD) -- a counter rebel movement organized by the United States against the then government of Liberia headed by after 1997.

The United States feared that Taylor, because of his relations with France shortly after his inauguration as president in 1997, might use his National Patriotic Front of Liberia (NPFL) fighters to attack US-controlled mining interests in Guinea. Subsequently, in 2000-2001, when rebels believed to be part of Taylor's NPFL fighters attacked Guinean villages along the borders with Liberia and Sierra Leone, the United States eventually provided substantial military assistance, weapons and ammunitions to the Guinea army to counter-attack strategic locations across the Liberian border in retaliation.

The seriousness of this threat to US interests was emphasized in a December 2001 communiqué issued by the US embassy in Conakry which stated in part: "unrest in Guinea does not only represent a major security problem for West Africa but also our nation's security because the United States has invested heavily in Guinea where our strategic interests remain strong and multi-faceted."

In 2003, the United States and its imperialist allies implemented a new tactic in their efforts to protect the mining concessions of its two most leading North American corporations, Alcan and Alcoa. The Guinean Ministry of Mineral Resources granted the richest aluminum-mining concession in West Africa to a Japanese corporation, Global Aluminum Productions Corporation (GAPCO), a subsidiary of Mitsubishi and Merubeni conglomerates. This agreement allowed GAPCO the definitive right to undertake exploration and extraction of aluminum resources around the Sangaredi area for a period of hundred years.

This annoyed the United States and its allies, whose control of Guinea's aluminum resources since 1984 had depended on Alcoa and Alcan's monopoly over mineral exploitation in the country. In retaliation, the United States withdrew its supposed assistance and support to the Conte regime and alternatively sought a new agenda for regime change in Guinea. Because of absolute loyalty to the regime and due to excessive military spending, senior officers within the Guinean military had grown extremely rich from misappropriation of salaries and did not think of overthrowing Conte. A coup plot in January 2005, believed to have been masterminded through the US embassy in Conakry, failed to topple Conte, resulting in the dismissal of several officers.

Realizing that a military coup is a difficult sell to an army that is doggedly loyal to the presidency, the US began targeting disaffected opposition parties. However, the various opposition leaders - Ba Mamadou, a former World Bank consultant, Sidya Toure, an ex-employee of the IMF, and Prof. Alpha Conde, a retired lecturer at Sorbonne University in France, persuaded by the US to form an opposition coalition in a campaign against Conte - couldn't overturn the Conte regime as was envisaged by the US. Opposition leaders lacked the required mass support to carry out a popular agenda and were unwilling to accept the leadership of any one of them. Undeterred in its plans to carry out its regime change agenda, the US changed focus to the labor unions and a section of the civil society movement.

Consequently, in a report issued by USAID on Guinea's political situation in June 2005, the United States openly called on the European Union and international financial institutions to withhold aid and assistance to Guinea as a way of forcing the Conte regime to embark on "democratic reforms."

In the three years subsequent to the GAPCO agreement, the US expended around a million dollars in a program designed to prepare labor union leadership for a mass campaign against Conte. It was this strategy that ultimately culminated in the trade unionists position during the mass uprisings against the Conte regime in January and February of this year. This also explains the trade union leadership's decision to suggest the appointment of Lansana Kouyate, a US neocolonialist, as Guinea's new prime minister.

The fact that the trade unionist position was part of the wider sinister plot by the United States and its corporate allies are clearly evident in a statement issued by the State Department following Kouyate's appointment. It reads:

"The United States notes with satisfaction the appointment on March 28, 2007 of a new government of broad consensus in Guinea. We salute Prime Minister Lansana Kouyate's intention to focus priorities on macroeconomic stability... The new government provides Guinea an important opportunity to improve democratic governance through increased transparency and the protection of human rights. We look forward to working with the new government as they translate their strategy for a democratic, accountable and prosperous Guinea into action."

The deep involvement of the US in the Guinea crisis and the reality that the trade union leadership received directives from the American embassy in Conakry is further evident in a statement issued by the embassy on February 16, 2007, which condemned the Conte regime while also expressing dissatisfaction regarding the desperate actions of the masses who no longer followed the dictates of the labor union leaders.

It is this imperialist conspiracy executed by fickle minded petty bourgeois sellouts that necessitated the imposition of Kouyate as leader of a neocolonial government responsible for securing the interests of American corporations in Guinea. So, it is inarguable that Kouyate is not a consensus prime minister as the middle class media has been suggesting. And it would be irrational, naïve and preposterous to assume or suggest that the struggle of the masses in Guinea to reclaim control of the country's immense natural resources has been nipped in the bud following a middle class settlement that insultingly imposes an imperialist puppet on the blood of the masses.

In fact, current trends within Guinea and the region in general pose a serious threat to the ability of the regime to continuously hold the people hostage under a suffocating and decadent system. Kouyate is faced with tremendous contradictions, as seventy-five percent of the country has absolutely refused to recognize his legitimacy. In most parts of the interior, his authority is non-existent and, worst still, within Conakry he confronts the rifles of angry soldiers who are still loyal to Conte. There is serious bad blood between Kouyate and Conte's old political clique who has become isolated and represents another danger from within.

Kouyate's only hopes – hopes which he shares with his imperialist masters – is the employment of military power, and in this case, the deployment of an international military force that will create space for the enforcement of a deceitful electoral process to "legitimize" this ongoing process.

This is the main reason why Kouyate visited the United States to meet with the Bush regime and officials of the World Bank and IMF. In an interview with *All Africa Global Media* in Washington, he clearly indicated the seriousness of US involvement in the situation in Guinea. He said:

"The immediate need of my government is to rehabilitate all the destroyed buildings inside the country, because without that we cannot send the local authorities to establish and monitor election procedures. But, immediately, we need money. The European Union has committed roughly seven million euros, but this is directly linked to the election process itself. It has nothing to do with the rehabilitation or restoration of the buildings we are talking about, which will require some money. So I discussed that today with the newly appointed ambassador of the United States to Conakry. The policy of "wait and see" in emergency cases is not a good option. The situation can deteriorate. It is wise to help before the election. Secretary Rice said the United States was going to help us as soon as possible."

A few days after Kouyate's visit, a US Navy frigate was dispatched to the coast of Conakry. In a press conference held on June 22, 2007 by the US embassy in Conakry, the Commanding Officer Michael Elliott told journalists in Conakry, "the deployment is part of an ongoing effort to enhance relations throughout West Africa and the US commitment to help bring stability and economic opportunity to the region." The vessel, an Oliver Hazard Perry Guided Missile Fast Frigate, is home ported in Mayport, Florida, and has been operating in the region for several weeks.

A statement issued by the Africanist Movement this week concludes that the development in Guinea represents a serious threat and challenge to the African liberation movement. The Africanist Movement insists that the struggle in Guinea is not over. Africanist leaders emphasize that efforts against neocolonialism in Conakry represent a strategic component of the general struggle for African independence and control over the continent's vast resources. It is a clear call to the international African community, revolutionaries and progressives around the world to unite in defense of a just struggle for self-determination.

CHAPTER 10

SIERRA LEONE: ELECTIONS AND MIDDLE CLASS CRISIS

Ahmed Tejan Kabbah of the Sierra Leone Peoples Party (SLPP) came to power in Sierra Leone following general elections held in 1996. His presidency occurred at a time when the country was faced with a raging civil war, which had been ongoing for five years. Kabbah was to serve eleven years as President in the midst of a rebellious national army and the rebels of Foday Sankoh's Revolutionary United Front (RUF). He left power in 2007 following an election in which the All Peoples Congress (APC) of Ernest Bai Koroma defeated his party, the Sierra Leone Peoples Party (SLPP). In this article, first published a week before the election run-off in August 2007 by the Africanist Bulletin, Chernoh Alpha M. Bah analyzes the elections and predicts that the SLPP will be defeated by the APC. The article also concludes that the pending APC victory will create more misery for the people. Apart from its prophetic note, the article highlights the crisis that the elections of 2007 created for the middle class politicians in Sierra Leone and its wider implications for the aspirations of the masses to be free from poverty and the other contradictions resulting from the failures of the current political arrangement of the country. It also shows how the ethno-regional divisions of the country define the nature and character of political struggle in Sierra Leone.

Sierra Leone's president, Ahmed Tejan Kabbah has threatened to declare a state of emergency ahead of the election run-off to be held this week if violence between supporters of contending parties persists. Already there have been continuous reports of violent clashes over the last few days in several towns and villages in the south and east of the country among supporters of rival political parties, forcing the police to declare a dawn to dusk curfew in most areas across the country.

The run-off presidential elections will be held between the opposition All Peoples Congress (APC) leader Ernest Koroma and incumbent ruling party candidate Solomon Ekuma Berewa. Berewa is also Kabbah's vice president.

The opposition APC won a majority of the parliamentary seats during the first round of voting (44%), followed by the incumbent SLPP (38%). The Peoples Movement for Democratic Change (PMDC) trails behind by a wide margin (14%). To win, a candidate must garner 55% of the vote. The SLPP, which has been in power since 1996 with Kabbah as its leader, cannot afford to lose the elections. Kabbah and his cronies in the SLPP are determined to hold onto political power.

The APC leadership, having lost political power in 1992 due to a military coup , sees the current elections as the best opportunity to assume leadership of the country and is exploiting the desperate and genuine desire of the masses for political and economic transformation to accomplish its selfish power objective.

Ironically, the current electoral success of the APC does not result from a new political program that differs from that of the incumbent party, thereby offering hope to the poor and exploited masses in Sierra Leone. Instead, its achievement can be attributed, in part, to the lack of a viable alternative. The APC has never been such an alternative and will never be. In fact, none of the current existing political parties offer real, honest leadership to the electorate. In such a desolate political landscape, people are naturally compelled to choose a perceived lesser evil.

There is no fundamental difference between the SLPP and APC or any of the existing political parties participating in the current political process. All of the political parties participating in the election, particularly the SLPP and APC, originate from and represent various sectors of a corrupt middle class that sees political power as the license for personal aggrandizement and wealth accumulation. There is no exception to this dismal scenario even with the Peoples Movement for Democratic Change (PMDC), which was founded in 2005.

The circumstances that gave rise to the formation and existence of these political groupings and their objectives have always remained the same. The PMDC, formed and led by Charles Margai, only increased the crisis within the ruling elite. Margai, a former SLPP Internal Affairs Minister in the current regime, broke ranks with the SLPP after he was denied the party leadership in the 2005 delegates' conference in which Berewa was elected or imposed as presidential candidate of the party for the 2007 elections. Berewa was never a suitable and popular candidate within the rank and file of the SLPP but his nomination is said to have been influenced by Kabbah, who desired to have his vice president succeed him. Berewa appears to be a party loyalist, one that is likely to defend and maintain Kabbah's current policies. It is this desire to have a loyalist succeed him that led Kabbah to impose Berewa as his successor, first within the SLPP and later on the country. It is this situation that resulted in the split within the SLPP and ultimately led to the formation of the PMDC. Margai, a son of Sierra Leone's former prime minister, claims that his resignation from the Kabbah government and the SLPP is based on widespread corruption and lack of transparency within the party and government.

An unfortunate aspect of the political system in most African countries, including Sierra Leone, is that, during and after the "independence period", the formation of political parties took an ethnic-regional divide. The current political divide between the northwest and southeast is a colonial construct arising out of the British constitutional arrangement of 1947, originally designed to create a divide between the "Creole" of the colony and the so-called "natives" of the protectorate. This colonial strategy was designed to weaken the militant, anti-colonial movement that had developed among certain sections of the "Creole" community that later gave rise to the formation of the SLPP in 1952 under the leadership of Milton Margai. Historically, the SLPP is an offspring of the general imperialist strategy after 1945 that ensured the transfer of political power to neocolonialist conservatives following the destruction of the anti-colonial movement led by Wallace-Johnson.

The inter-party struggles and leadership acrimony that developed within the SLPP prior to the 1957 elections and during the 1960 constitutional conference in London resulted, first, in the formation of the Peoples National Party (PNP) led by Albert Margai (father of PMDC leader Charles Margai) and, second, in the Election Before Independence Movement (EBIM), which later became the APC under the leadership of Siaka Stevens. Present political parties in Sierra Leone have arisen out of similar splits and power struggles among different sectors of the petty bourgeoisie for control of the state.

The division within the ruling class elite has had serious negative impacts on the broader mass of the country. It has fragmented national unity and reinforced false ethnic patriotism and regional consciousness among the masses. Traditionally, the SLPP had long relied on the south and east, mostly inhabited by Mendes, for support. The Mendes constitute the largest ethnic group in the country. The APC, on the other hand, relies on the north and west, predominantly inhabited by Temnes and Limbas, for its support. Whereas other political parties had emerged from among the northern ethnic groups, the south and east had always remained SLPP strongholds. This is why the formation of the PMDC had significant effects on the chances of the SLPP in the current elections. Split within the SLPP has meant a split of the votes from the traditional strongholds of the party. Of the 112 contested seats in parliament the APC had won 59, the SLPP 43 and PMDC 10 during the first round of voting. With a run-off scheduled between the SLPP and APC, PMDC leader Charles Margai has thrown his support to the APC ultimately reducing Berewa's chances of victory.

But the central questions are: why can't Kabbah and his SLPP cronies afford to lose the presidential elections? And more importantly, what will an APC victory mean to the aspirations of the masses?

The truth of the matter is that the current SLPP leadership is jittery, in part, because its policies have not translated into any form of development in the country. They completely ignored the welfare and interest of the masses that voted them into power. Although Kabbah came to power in 1996 following the national campaign for democracy, his eleven years in office has meant increased imperialist and multinational penetration of the country. In his quest to maintain power, Kabbah gave out strategic mining concessions to several multinational British and American mining corporations in exchange for military services and protection. A British mercenary firm, Sandline International was contracted under an agreement signed between Kabbah and the British government to provide military equipment and training for the Civil Defense Forces (CDF), a militia group established by the SLPP, to fight for the restoration of Kabbah's government after he was overthrown in a military coup in 1997. This agreement allowed the use of an international military intervention force that claimed the lives of thousands of innocent people to restore the SLPP government then exiled in Guinea Conakry.

Today, Branch Energy, a British corporation tied to Sandline International, mines the most lucrative diamond concession in West Africa as part of that arrangement. Other corporations like Mile Stone, Africa Gold and Diamonds Ltd, Petrograd Mines, Koidu Holdings, Sandoh Minerals, Sierra Leone Diamond Company (SLDC), which is now African Minerals, and Bridge Resources are among some ninety multinational corporations currently exploiting resources in Kono located in eastern Sierra Leone. It is estimated that about 10 million carats of diamonds is being taken out of Kono every month through the activities of these corporations. Sadly, while these corporations are making huge profits, people in Sierra Leone live on less than a dollar a day with no electricity, no good roads, no pipe borne water, no proper health care system and other social services. The economic infrastructure necessary for growth and development is non-existent.

During Kabbah's presidency, a sophisticated counterinsurgency program was introduced into the country, facilitated by massive police recruitment and the deployment of imperialist troops and intelligence agencies. A program of structural adjustment influenced by imperialist nations was also adopted. For instance, the British maintain a military base and huge military presence in the country and the FBI had an outpost in Freetown. The British, through the International Military Advisory Training Team (IMATT), are in charge of training and restructuring the military and defense policy of the country. British military officers, who command British troops in Sierra Leone, and police officers, dominate the Office of National Security, which is similar to the British MI6. A situation where foreigners are placed in charge of Sierra Leone's national intelligence and security existed.

On the economic front, the British Department for International Development (DFID) – the equivalent of the United States Agency for International Development (USAID) – regulated the economic program of the country. The justice sector reform program also necessitated the appointment of British judges into the justice department.

Low life expectancy, high infant and maternal mortality rates, a rapidly declining economy and a vastly hungry population were the products of Kabbah's policies and eleven years in office. His intention was to arguably continue and sustain these policies through the imposition of Berewa as president of the country.

Clearly, the imperialist strategy not only protected the neocolonial Kabbah regime, but it also confused the masses regarding the root cause of their problems. Imperialists have always used corruption and flagrant misuse of public resources as a blind to explain the causes of poverty and underdevelopment in most African countries, whereas the actual causes are neocolonial state exploitation and oppression. The SLPP government of Kabbah is one of the most corrupt neocolonial regimes on the continent, and it had used these imperialist funded strategies and programs to suppress would be contending opposition elements even within the middle class.

For instance, the United Nations-backed Special Court for Sierra Leone, established under an arrangement between the SLPP government and United Nations for the trial of individuals believed to bear the greatest responsibility for crimes committed during the ten years war, is being used by the SLPP and the imperialists to silence perceived threats to their interests in the region. Among those indicted by the Special Court are former leaders of the Civil Defense Forces (CDF), the militia organization trained and armed by the British through the Sandline arrangement to restore the government of Kabbah after the military coup of 1997. The Civil Defense Forces (CDF) leader, Sam Hinga Norman was Kabbah's Deputy Defense Minister during the period of the conflict and later Internal Affairs Minister at the time of his arrest by the Special Court. CDF members have argued that Kabbah should equally be indicted because he was the head of the CDF War Council and Defense Minister simultaneously, under whose directives Hinga Norman headed the operations of the CDF. PMDC leader Charles Margai, a professional lawyer, had functioned as one of the defense lawyers for the CDF leaders indicted by the Special Court.

However, Norman died early this year, under controversial circumstances, as a detainee of the Special Court. But before his death, Norman and other CDF detainees at the Special Court purportedly wrote a statement requesting their members and supporters to vote the PMDC. Margai had used this to garner support from former CDF members and supporters of the late Hinga Norman in the run-up to the elections. It is this CDF membership within the PMDC, mostly ex-militia fighters that have engaged the SLPP in open battles in the south and east of the country resulting in burning of houses. The APC itself appears to have utilized the same tactic by incorporating renegades of the RUF and disbanded soldiers of the old army into its rank and file.

Consequently, with an opposition majority in the parliament and an APC-PMDC alliance ahead of the presidential run-off, Kabbah and his SLPP stalwarts have become extremely worried. Apart from fear of losing vested interests in the multinational corporate exploitation of the nation's resources, Kabbah risks being taken to the Special Court. Most SLPP ministers would also have to face tribunals and commissions of enquiry that will be established through the influence of the APC-PMDC merger. This may also have implications for the large multinational interests in the country and represents a threat to the corrupt patronage network that has developed between the current ruling class elite and mercantile class, predominantly Lebanese, Asiatic, Fulani and other indigenous business magnates who have become prosperous during the last few years due to rogue relations with this political mafia.

Regardless of the outcome of the current elections, the situation of the masses will remain dire. Endemic, institutionalized corruption over the years has resulted in the development of a rogue middle class that has grown extremely wealthy in the midst of massive poverty and wretchedness. The statistics on growth and development have remained abysmal for the last forty-six years of neocolonial state terror much of it perpetrated during the more than two decades of APC rule. So regardless of who wins the current political contest, there will be no significant policy change that will reverse the current trend. If anything, poverty and backwardness will only increase due to endemic corruption and organized state exploitation.

Perhaps the most encouraging trend in the midst of this political free-for-all is the potential of growth of political consciousness among the masses. The seemingly endless struggles among the petty bourgeoisie for political power to selfishly accumulate wealth, political corruption, state oppression and neocolonial exploitation have not only resulted in severe crisis within the middle class, but have also increased the aspirations of the masses for revolutionary change. It has stimulated political agitation among the people and fueled their desire for change in their material conditions. People are rapidly becoming conscious that decades of organized state oppression and exploitation have denied them access to state resources and social services necessary to change their conditions of existence. They are coming to terms with the necessity of building a working class revolutionary movement that will fight to overturn the existing status quo.

CHAPTER 11

BRITAIN'S CORPORATE AGENDA IN SIERRA LEONE

President Ernest Bai Koroma of Sierra Leone came to power following the general elections of 2007 in which his party, the All Peoples Congress (APC), defeated the incumbent ruling party at the time, the Sierra Leone Peoples Party (SLPP). The APC returned to power fifteen years after it was overthrown in a coup in 1992. The SLPP claimed that the APC's victory was orchestrated by the United Nations Special Representative to the country, Victor Angelo, who they alleged engineered a program of regime change in the country. The SLPP's candidate in the elections, Solomon Ekuma Berewa, maintained that the international community never wanted him to become Sierra Leone's president. He was the vice president and would have succeeded Tejan Kabbah if, according to him, the elections were not rigged. Following allegations of over-voting, the National Electoral Commission (NEC) disqualified more than 477 polling stations in SLPP strongholds in the east of the country. In this article published immediately after the elections, Chernoh Alpha M. Bah's analyzes the Ernest Koroma government. Bah argues that Ernest Koroma's program will surely deepen multinational interests in Sierra Leone. He examines Ernest Koroma's economic program and contends that it signals the beginning of a new neo-liberal agenda that will worsen the conditions of the people.

A recent statement issued by the British Department for International Development (DFID) revealed that England has provided some US$72 million to support what it refers to as "a new social and economic reform program" in Sierra Leone, to be carried out by the new regime of Ernest Bai Koroma.

Britain's Secretary of State for International Development, Douglas Alexander, said the money is part of Britain's "renewed assistance to the government of Sierra Leone now headed by Ernest Bai Koroma" and designed to "help the government carry out the implementation of policies that will maximize revenue as part of a new national recovery plan." This announcement is the result of discussions between Ernest Koroma and officials of the British government following his recent visit to London as a guest of British Prime Minister Gordon Brown and Queen Elizabeth II.

In a presentation held at Chatham House (formerly the Royal Institute for International Affairs) during his visit to London, Ernest Koroma told British politicians and multinationals that his government is committed to a "corporate agenda," one that will provide guarantees for multinational investment and exploitation.

Assuring the British political class of his willingness to carry out their dictates, Ernest Koroma re-echoed his inaugural statement that his government's intention is to run Sierra Leone as a corporation. His administration would be organized and run like a corporation with himself as the General Manager and his ministers as departmental heads providing guidance and support to multinationals who will occupy a shareholder status in the affairs of the country.

He called on Britain's capitalists to take advantage of the opportunity provided them in the transformation of Sierra Leone into a limited liability company now called "Sierra Leone Limited" saying, "The success of this vision depends on international partnership with England who has remained supportive of Sierra Leone political dispensation over the years."

Ernest Koroma also vowed to the British political class that his government would continue to provide security and guarantees for both British corporations and multinationals intending to venture into Sierra Leone and those already operating in the country as part of his "government's new agenda."

A reassured Britain throws support behind Koroma's regime

Consequently, it is unsurprising that, subsequent to Ernest Koroma's London visit, the British re-echoed their continuous commitment to maintaining the status quo in Sierra Leone by providing support to the newly imposed neocolonial government.

As a matter of fact, Koroma's ascension to power was overtly facilitated by Britain, the United States and the various western multinational corporations engaged in the theft and plunder of the country's resources. The fact that the British and their imperialist allies, in favor of Ernest Koroma's All Peoples Congress (APC), fraudulently rigged the elections in Sierra Leone is no longer an issue of debate.

Subsequently, several British corporations and multinational financial organizations immediately developed a sophisticated international public relations strategy aimed not only at lending credence to the fraudulent electoral process but also to showcase Sierra Leone as a bastion of stable democracy with endless marketing opportunities conducive for international financial investments.

The imperialist media employed the theatrical concept of make-believe as a political tactic to anoint Ernest Koroma as the new democratic statesman in Africa. They put him forward as the opposition leader who supposedly enjoyed the mass support necessary to win an election against a hated incumbent.

Lesser of two evils?

The reality is that those who appeared to appreciate Ernest Koroma's supposed success in past elections are not convinced that he has answers to the numerous problems facing the poor and exploited masses or that the political program he promotes differs from that of the Sierra Leone People's Party (SLPP). Koroma just appeared to be, at that moment, the only alternative between two proportionate evils.

It should be remembered that, leading up to the elections, the Kabbah government that Ernest Koroma replaced had become hugely unpopular and hated by the masses because of its neglect of the people's welfare and interests. In order to continue in power, Kabbah needed increased imperialist and multinational presence in the country, which eventually isolated the people from their own resources, leaving them without the capital required for growth and development.

Low life expectancy, high infant and maternal mortality rates, a rapidly declining economy and a vastly hungry population became the hallmarks of Kabbah's policies and eleven years in office. Such a violently hostile situation will nurture seeds of mass discontent inimical to the existence of the "peaceful environment" needed for multinational corporate activities and the operations of international finance.

British and North American corporations hold huge stakes in the economic activities of the country and therefore require security and protection for their corporate interests and multinational investments in Sierra Leone.

Realizing the frustration of the masses against the SLPP under Kabbah and the potential threat posed by increased Chinese influence and economic ventures in the country, the British and their imperialist allies felt the severe threats that their large multinational interests faced needed to be countered. This played a major factor in the imperialist maneuvers to rig past elections in favor of Koroma and the APC.

Continuing misery was expected under Koroma

Prior to this election, however, we pointed out that regardless of the outcome, the situation of the African masses in Sierra Leone would still remain insufferable. We knew that there would be no significant changes in policies that would reverse the trend of affairs experienced under Kabbah's SLPP government.

The fact of the matter is that this policy of "corporate colonialism" has resulted in endemic, institutionalized corruption, which in turn developed a rogue middle class that sees political power as an instrument for the salvation of themselves and their families at the expense of the masses.

This is why Ernest Koroma's decision to transform Sierra Leone into a corporation is the climax of a neocolonial, capitalist exploitative tendency stage-managed by Britain, the United States and their various multinational corporations who profit from the numerous resources in the country. It is a political and economic strategy designed to enhance easy access and monopoly over the resources of the country by western capitalist corporations through the enactment of policies that favor a range of guarantees and tax incentives. It strengthens the protective relationship that already exists between the middle class political elites and the huge multinational finance representatives guarded by the various British and United States counterintelligence agencies and secret security services currently stationed in the country. It is classic neo-liberalism that puts every sector of the country on auction to the highest bidder, and where "profit" and "capital regeneration" are prioritized at the expense of the welfare of the masses.

Sierra Leone sold to the highest bidder

In the last few weeks following Koroma's return from England, several delegations representing huge British multinational interests flooded the country, negotiating for various concessions. These have included a "high powered" British business delegation representing the London Mining Company, which has concluded agreements recently with Koroma's regime to carry out mining in the iron ore mining reserves at Lunsar and Marampa in the north of the country.

Koroma's regime regards multinational corporate interventions as key towards the achievement of his neocolonial objectives and realization of his "corporate agenda." The western governments see Ernest Koroma's "corporate agenda" as a potential tool in curtailing growing Chinese influence and economic ventures in the country. Very recently, a British-owned timber logging company is believed to have influenced Ernest Koroma's decision to ban Chinese logging companies from the country's forests. Although Koroma claimed that his decision was influenced by environmental concerns, reports have indicated that his Ministry of Forestry and the Environment is engaged in negotiations with several British and American companies interested in logging.

Consequently, while multinationals continue to flood the country, the conditions of the masses have grown worse than they were under Kabbah's SLPP. Barely four months after the elections, the country been hit twice by severe shortages in petroleum products and foodstuffs.

During the last two months, the country has witnessed over seven different strikes from workers in various government departments over non-payment of salaries and politically motivated sackings of their colleagues. At the same time, prices of basic commodities including rice, flour, palm oil, groundnuts and other food provisions have skyrocketed, experiencing price increases of over fifty percent. High import and export duties recently imposed by Koroma's APC regime in its desperation to extract domestic revenue have severely destabilized investments of indigenous commercial ventures. Scarcity and price escalation resulting from this economic crisis has enabled the huge multinationals that monopolize the various sectors of trade and commerce in the country to enjoy alarming profits.

Solution for masses is power in own hands

The anxiety and expectations that accompanied Ernest Koroma's ascension to power in 2007 are rapidly vanishing from the minds of those who hoped that an APC victory would automatically transform the harsh conditions they face. People are quickly realizing that Koroma and his APC are no different from the preceding Kabbah government. Both groups belong to the same soup.

This is where an alternative political program becomes the answer. Freedom from this situation of exploitation and oppression will only come through the organized efforts of workers and peasants. Workers and peasants need a program that addresses their needs and aspirations, one that helps them realize their class interests. The African working class can only free itself from this situation through the overthrow of the existing social system. The actualization of this process is the task and responsibility of revolutionaries and progressives.

CHAPTER 12

PRESIDENT KOROMA: A PATH TOWARDS AUTHORITARIAN DEMOCRACY IN SIERRA LEONE

The following essay is a combination of series of opinion articles published during the month of May 2013, addressing key political questions dealing with the practice of democracy, the exercise of presidential power, police violence, brutality, and matters of constitutional review in Sierra Leone. In this essay, Chernoh Alpha M. Bah expresses lack of faith in President Ernest Bai Koroma's claim to good governance and democracy. Highlighting the collapse of democratic values, the abuse of political power by the police, and other state institutions since the All Peoples Congress (APC) of President Koroma assumed power in 2007, Chernoh Alpha M. Bah argues that political corruption, suppression of democratic rights, injustice, and disregard for the rule of law have become rampant in the country with the advent of President Koroma's leadership. Using key issues such as the outcome of the 2013 APC National Convention, the review of the 1991 Constitution, and the detention of politicians amongst the opposition, Chernoh Alpha M. Bah concludes that President Koroma and his All Peoples Congress (APC) are not only undermining the democratic values of the country but also plotting to perpetuate a monopoly of power in Sierra Leone. At the core of this essay is the question of injustice and repression against opposition politicians, political sycophancy and rank opportunism characteristic of the administration and President Koroma's zest in abusing the instruments of state power. These developments, he concludes, typify tendencies of authoritarian democracy. The essay also blames the opposition politicians and their parties for the state of affairs in the country.

The 2013 Convention of the All Peoples Congress (APC) and its endorsement of President Ernest Koroma as the party's chairman and leader created a huge debate across Sierra Leone. It is a debate that was anchored on key questions: the future of democracy, the issue of constitutional review, the role of opposition parties, the police and the rule of law in Sierra Leone.

The fact that President Koroma was the only candidate for the party's highest position in the convention of the APC was not the only factor that triggered the debate. It was also caused by the question of constitutional review and the idea that President Ernest Bai Koroma was intending to seek another presidential term outside of the requirements of the national constitution. What became apparent from the response to this development was the question of constitutionality and adherence to democratic practice. Is the APC committed to democracy? Is Koroma's leadership of the country a cancer to democracy? To answer these questions, one has to put into proper perspective the issues that generated the discussion itself. A clear examination of recent developments in the country before and immediately after the APC convention will offer a helpful understanding of the path that the country is taking.

The Third Term Agenda

Before the convention, some APC partisans took over the national media to argue that Ernest Bai Koroma deserved another term in office. Without being clear whether the campaign for "another term in office" was for their party or the country, APC propagandists created serious alarms in the minds of pro-democratic forces across the country.

They gave the impressions that Koroma was planning to seek another term in the next presidential elections. In fact, senior APC members who were very close to Koroma were the ones who took this nauseating discussion to the public domain. They argue, rather sycophantically and hypocritically, that the president should be rewarded again because in their opinion, he is the best that has happened to the country in fifty years. Whether these usual praise-singers were sent by the president to sound public opinion on the question was unclear. But Koroma, on whose behalf they appear to be speaking, remained perfectly silent on the issue. When it emerged that many of the APC delegates at the convention in Freetown were going to "re-appoint" or "coronate" him as their party leader again, suspicions became widespread. Many people were left in wonderment. They started to ask whether the president was just interested in another term as leader of the APC. Was the extended party leadership a prelude to a third term bid for the president? How does this development relate to the question of reviewing the national constitution?

No official answers were initially provided by the president's office on these serious democratic questions. Pro-democratic forces, largely found in the opposition ranks, were increasingly concerned over such developments. Along street corners and the popular "ataya bases" across the city, ordinary people whom the

APC claimed to represent – were also equally worried about the future of democracy in the country.

People had expected Koroma to use the convention to clarify the suspicions that he intended to seek a third term in the next presidential elections. Instead of transparency, the president's address to the APC delegates created much doubt in the minds of ordinary people. It tacitly agreed with suggestions from his many propagandists and praise singers that a third term bid would be a welcome idea to him. A pro-Koroma columnist had argued that opposition to a third term bid for the president should be dismissed because "an extension of President Koroma's current term may be necessitated by the process of constitutional review and change in such a manner as to prescribe an extension to the current five year term to which the president is limited." If this is to be taken seriously, then we must ask the question: is the ongoing constitutional review geared towards changing the presidential term of office to accommodate Koroma's bid for a third term? Another pro-APC newspaper had gone even further to ascertain that "APC's third term is one hundred percent confirmed." The newspaper reported, "the APC will be re-elected for its third term in office because of the high note on which the party is carrying out its development activities across the Nation."

While both arguments took a different approach to the same question, their conclusions are premised from identical standpoints. They both believe that because of the so-called "development projects" that the government was reportedly undertaking across the country, the APC should be rewarded with another term in office. Although there were different positions about how that "third term" should be actualized, two things stand out clearly from both lines of the argument as reflected in the two positions referred to above.

First, there was a section of the ruling party who strongly believed that the APC's image and face is that of President Koroma. They also believed that all "achievements" within the first five years were solely those of Koroma and not that of the party and therefore the president must be accorded another term of office. This group does not foresee the APC surviving an electoral contest without Koroma as its figure head. Second, there is another group of APC members who equally believe that the APC should stay in office because of its so-called "national development programs" but this should not happen with Koroma as its frontrunner. This group believed that the "amount of development exported to the south-east" of the country is enough to make the APC win repeatedly in any electoral contest with or without Koroma. These two tendencies run concurrently within the party.

These are questions that the APC convention failed to clarify. Where do we draw the line between those who believe in a third term for the APC with Koroma as the frontrunner and those who want a third term for the APC without Koroma? Where is President Koroma in all of this? Is the president really interested in a third term for himself?

Although Koroma's position on this question was officially unknown, rumors that he intended to stay for another term were made extremely rife by the utterances of the many sycophants and opportunists who floated around him. The fact that some of these opportunists hanging around the president had gone on public platforms saying he deserves "a third term" without any rebuttal from the president's office was highly problematic. And it portends serious dangers for the stability of the country's growing democracy.

What the protagonists of the so-called "third term agenda of president Koroma" failed to consider was the fact that the legitimacy of the current second term of the president was still being challenged by a majority of the democratic forces in the country. It was therefore senseless for someone to assert that Koroma deserves another term in office when protest against his acquisition of a second term was before the Supreme Court. Consequently, it was completely incomprehensible that APC propagandists and Koroma's praise-singers in particular would seek to introduce such a suffocating idea at that material time.

The presidential term should not be the subject of a debate centered on the extension of the mandate of a sitting president. We should not talk of reviewing the constitution because a few individuals want to create room for Koroma to stay for another term. There is no democratic tradition in the world that rewards leaders with perpetuity because their political record is assumed to be unblemished. This is why, when APC propagandists address Koroma as a saint and messiah, they don't realize that they are exposing the excessive sycophancy and rank opportunism that typifies the political landscape since Koroma assumed power.

The questions they leave unanswered are always there staring at them in the face. These questions surround the most tormenting issues facing ordinary people across the country. Why is the president's leadership not free from the sins of political corruption, bribery, opposition poaching, police brutality and theft of public resources? Why has Koroma not solved the salary problems of teachers and university lecturers who are still owed bulks of backlog pays that calculators can no longer compute? Why is youth unemployment still on the increase?

APC propagandists claimed that the situation had been extremely good for the ordinary people in the last few years since Koroma assumed power. But the truth is that the living conditions of ordinary people grew worse at supersonic speed every day. Meanwhile, the APC partisans grew extremely wealthy due to rogue political and ethnic alliances. These are the rank opportunists and political sycophants who surround the president. They are the usual praise singers who are convinced that the president could get away with a third term bid. This is the group of opportunists and praise singers that backed the extension of Koroma's leadership for another term. This situation is now open to various interpretations.

The Constitutional Review

When the government announced that a review of the 1991 Constitution of Sierra Leone was about to commence, key fundamental questions were raised. These key questions had to be addressed if the constitutional review was to serve the national interest. Is the time appropriate to discuss a constitutional review? Is the government, under the leadership of Koroma, better positioned to lead an exercise to review the constitution? Is the constitutional review going to be transparent and utterly democratic? What are the underlying motives behind the proposed constitutional amendments? Will the proposed amendments enhance open democratic participation? How are we going to ensure that the process includes mass participation and serves the interests of the broader sector of the country's population?

The people agreed that the 1991 Constitution needed to be reviewed to cater for the current socio-economic and political challenges presented by the new demographic and ethnographic realities of the country. But the most contentious issue was the fact that the discourse around a constitutional review occurred at a time when the country was under a government controlled by the All Peoples Congress (APC). This also posed the question: should the current APC government, under Koroma, be trusted to spearhead a review of the 1991 Constitution? This question is most significant when one considers the historical perspective around which constitutional reviews or amendments have occurred in the country. It was the APC, for instance, that organized the constitutional amendment in 1971, which created an all-powerful executive presidency in the country. It was the same APC that also introduced the constructional amendments that created one-party rule in the country in 1978. The current constitution that was billed for review was also introduced by the APC in 1991.

Put into this historical context, one must ask the definitive question: why is Koroma only thinking of a constitutional review at this time? Was the constitutional review process a part of his manifesto in the 2012 elections? These questions have to be asked due to suspicions that the proposed constitutional review is either a part of an anti-democratic agenda by the APC partisans to place themselves in positions of power, or a plan to orchestrate a campaign for Koroma to bid for a third-term regardless of denials by the president's office. These suspicions have been strengthened by the fact that some APC party activists are still talking about a so-called third term for Koroma. Newspapers in Freetown recently reported that the APC Kailahun District executive had endorsed the president as party leader for 2017. This was even ahead of the party's 2013 convention. When the APC returned to power in 2007, some of the party's supporters boasted that they intend to stay in office for the next three decades. Although Koroma has announced that he does not intend to seek an additional term in office, the pronouncements of APC party activists and recent developments across the country gave this suspicion a fertile ground.

The APC is enthusiastic about staying in power to monopolize governance beyond 2017. Whether the party intends to do so with Ernest Bai Koroma at the helm of affairs remains to be seen. But the fact is that the APC of today can hardly divorce itself from the image and personality of Koroma. Party loyalists have said that the source of their relationship with the APC of today is the president. Even opposition politicians who defected to the APC during the last 2012 campaigns – whether they were paid with cash, jobs, or a combination of both – had also cited the same reasons. They all claimed that Ernest Bai Koroma is the party's messiah and the best thing that has happened to the country. Some political analysts have even argued that the APC could only hold itself together today because of Koroma. From this backdrop, it will not be far-fetched to fear that in their quest to remain within the corridors of power, Koroma's henchmen will do everything possible to persuade him that he could get away with a third-term bid. Koroma, who is now in bed with political sycophants and rank opportunists, may want to use the proposed constitutional review as an opportunity to implement such a misguided idea.

In a country where hunger and poverty live side-by-side with more than ninety percent of the country's population, state actors with ill-gotten wealth can easily utilize the instruments of the state to corrupt any political process. This is especially true in a country like Sierra Leone, where governance has only enriched a few and protected the interests of a handful. Corruption is a political tactic well mastered by the APC and Koroma seems to apply it quite efficiently to subdue his opponents and curtail opposition to his policies and programs.

Today we can hardly talk of a vibrant civil society movement in the country, an active trade union movement, or a truly independent media that holds state actors accountable to the masses. The opposition parties are also not free from poaching and bribes from the political party in power. This is certainly not a healthy political environment to address a constitutional review.

Illicitly accumulated wealth from the public budget makes politicians drunk with power. They foolishly think that the country will be theirs alone to govern. This could be exactly true in a country like Sierra Leone, where a president who amasses stolen wealth and mostly surrounded by sycophants and political opportunists could become a cancer to democracy. The temptation to flout laws and the democratic processes results into a tendency to undermine national institutions, and eventually the very constitution of the country. Recent developments in Sierra Leone exemplify this scenario. Koroma and his party henchmen have gone ahead to amend a strategic provision of the constitution even when a Committee charged with reviewing the very constitution is in place. This was done with intent to further the APC's grip on power. The opposition members of parliament have been accused of haven accepted bribes to support the process. Ernest Koroma has used political power and the national resources to tame resentment to his style of governance through bribes and administrative appointments.

With the absence of genuine opposition, politically corrupt African presidents will easily force the courts, Electoral Commissions in their respective countries, the police force, and all other institutions to act according to the interests of the ruling party and its officials. They are never offended when the democratic ethos of the Constitution is thrown to the gutter to fulfill their selfish agendas. Undermining the democratic values of the country is more feasible for such leaders than solving the unemployment crisis facing young people who have been rendered impoverished by crooked public policies of the state. Are we not faced with such a situation already in Sierra Leone?

A Constitutional Review could only be meaningful if the national institutions and social organizations that are supposed to support such a process are allowed to participate freely without directives from State House. The State House should stay out of the process.

In the two decades since the current multi-party constitution was enacted, amendment following review is absolutely needed. This is because time and demography have made it necessary for the Constitution to be reviewed. There is absolute need to examine particularly those provisions of the Constitution that hinder open democratic participation. It is necessary to ensure that the political process is made much more inclusive in order to cater for all members of the body politic. To have an inclusive political process, the laws must support open democratic governance, a system that favors actual decentralization of social, and economic development that is absolutely free from partisan considerations. A system of laws must be enacted that answers to the demands for truly independent public institutions that address the questions of civil and political rights, welfare, industrialization, employment and social progress. This is what a constitution that is truly democratic ought to reflect. But there is no need for a constitution that seeks to eternally perpetuate the dominion of a single political party or an individual against others in society. Nor is there a need for a constitution that marginalizes and or places a significant minority to the absolute will and caprices of a so-called simple majority. This is why there should be active mass participation to review a constitution of a country. The process to do so must ensure that all voices in the political spectrum of the country are heard and catered to.

This is important not only for the peace, stability and national cohesion of a country, but it helps to heal existing divisions in a country where the questions of ethnological and geographical divisions are key factors of the political system itself. It will guarantee national ownership of the process and provides citizens with the basis for actual redress of expressed and unexpressed grievances. The proposed Constitutional Review must therefore not be left in the hands of the APC and Koroma's wishes and desires. Everybody must participate because democracy is about inclusivity and not exclusivity. Here then lies the role of the opposition politicians and their parties.

Democracy and the Role of Opposition Parties

Where is the place and role of the opposition in a democracy? This is a serious question that must be addressed. It is the primary responsibility of opposition groups to exert the necessary pressure on the state to safeguard the democratic values of a country. Matters of constitutionality cannot be discussed in vacuum without the involvement of the masses' organizations. These organizations can be broad-based and include the trade union movement, press union, students' movement, youth organizations, peasants' cooperative societies, farmers' associations, women's groups, and political parties themselves.

In today's democracies, civil society organizations, professional bodies and non-governmental organizations are also part of this national organizational arrangement. There are also lobbyist groups that fight for the interests of "big business" and multinationals. But the concern here is the actual groups of open political forces who are engaged in the battle for state power. What is the expected role of opposition parties within such a context? Are Sierra Leone's opposition parties fulfilling their role and purpose in the country?

Of course, there are ten political parties registered in Sierra Leone at the moment, but only two are currently represented in parliament. These are the All Peoples Congress (APC) and Sierra Leone Peoples Party (SLPP). The others have just simply gone comatose. Little is heard of them anymore. Their leaders are practically nowhere to be found after the last elections. Once the elections were over, these political leaders retreated to their unknown destinations; perhaps the very places they were before the elections. The cameras and tape recorders have disappeared from them. They have quickly faded from the memory of the ordinary people.

Quite recently, the only thing that was heard of them was the usual and expected news that a few angry members had gone to the media again. This time they were not fighting over leadership, but they were struggling over money. They want to share money meant for the development of their parties. Their grievances are focused on the leaders accused of stealing funds donated to them by President Goodluck Jonathan of Nigeria. It was all about corruption within the ranks of the opposition parties. The individual stories have been extremely hilarious, even though very seriously indicting. Some say their leaders forged minutes of meetings that were never held and used those minutes to secretly open Bank Accounts where their portion of the money was lodged. Others alleged that their party leaders have personally used the money without due permission from members. As usual, some of these angry party members, who felt cheated, went on radio stations calling for transparency within their parties and accountability from their leaders. The quarrels were once again picked up by a few journalists and reported in the press. The final news was that complaints have been made to the Political Parties Registration Commission (PPRC), the institution charged with the responsibility of regulating political party activities. The PPRC was reportedly looking into individual cases of how the monies were spent by the various political party leaders. Some party leaders informed the Commission that they used the said money to pay outstanding rents for their offices. One particular party leader was reported to have said that he used his party's own share of the funds to buy mini buses or "poda-poda" vans to start a commercial transport enterprise in Freetown.

This unfortunately has been the status of the so-called opposition parties in Sierra Leone. Weeks before the elections, they were actively talking and shouting against corruption and other aspects of bad governance. After the elections, they ceased to exist as political organizations and their executive members were tearing each other apart over party funds. It seems the elections for which they were formed were over and gone. They too have folded their files and packed their bags and headed home. They were simply constituted for the purposes of elections alone and once elections were over, they fold-up and head home. What next? They had to wait aimlessly until dates for the next general elections were announced.

Political party leaders in Sierra Leone have limited their operations to elections only. It seems their understanding of politics is fixed around the contest for votes alone. Their main focus is how to participate in elections and nothing else. For some party leaders, elections are a money making exercise in which they form alliances with the highest bidder. During election time, they conduct bargains, collect a few million Leones and announce support for one party candidate. Once the elections are over, some of them get appointed to strategic positions in government. Those who could not be appointed just retreat to their places of non-existence and wait till the next round of general elections again. In between then, they float around public offices to visit their comrades who are in government ministries and departments. They have to visit them occasionally or even regularly without official appointments because these officials owe them a debt for their support in the previous elections that gave them the jobs. The reasons for the unannounced visits, most times unwelcome, is to demand financial reward and a share of the stolen resources.

These are the individuals making up the political parties that exist in the country. They are made up of politicians whose business in politics is geared towards making money for themselves by any means. When they are in opposition, they collect bribes from officials of the party in power. When they are in power, they steal from the public budget. Then share a small portion of the looted resources with their friends in the opposition who supported them in the past elections that brought them to power. This is a typology of political corruption that has become rife in the country during the recent years with Koroma and his All Peoples Congress (APC) in power. This culture of political corruption has become seriously ingrained into the psyche of the politicians. It is a corrupt culture that transforms a poor ruling party organizer into an overnight million-aire due to suffocating ethno-political alliances. The activities of politicians in the country today are not free from the cancer of opportunism that such a political culture promotes. The mentality of the ordinary political activist in Sierra Leone today is governed by this notion of greed and pursuit of opportunistic ambitions. It is political culture that has made people to believe that, through the established political patronage network of the society, it is possible for a poor political activist to move from a match-box house in a poor working class neighborhood into a mansion at the affluent section of the city, if they are in the good books of the party in power.

This is why election is the only pre-occupation of the politicians. This is all they care for and are interested in. They use the elections to make money or get appointments and then open the gates to corruption. But the question is for how long will political parties in the country continue to operate within such an environment?

A political party that cannot organize anything outside of an electoral activity is not worthy of mass support. How can a party be a "mass party" if its entire program is centered on filling-in candidates for an electoral contest? For a party to win an electoral contest, it must first win the confidence of the masses and their loyalty and support. This can only happen if the party is actively engaged in the daily struggles of the people whether these struggles are over bread and butter, housing, education, and healthcare or workers' salaries.

The opposition parties in a democracy should always be on their feet champi-oning the causes of the masses. They should always be heard speaking in defense of the people and their right to better living conditions. An alternative to an existing status quo can only be seen if the opposition parties help the masses to see one. The opposition parties must always be seen as providing an alternative. Of what use is an opposition that is practically dormant and passive in the face of obvious excesses by officials of the ruling party?

Since the end of the last elections, little is heard from the many opposition parties registered to operate in the country. Even those who have representatives in parliament have been very silent on the questions facing ordinary people across the country. The only stories that make the headlines today relate to dinner parties organized for a visiting diplomat, the presidential awards at State House, or birth-day parties of ministers and their concubines. The other so-called development news constitutes government propaganda put out by ruling party praise singers. All of this is from the public budget and at the expense of the ordinary tax-payer.

But what can the opposition say in such a situation when it is largely fighting over party funds or engaged in meaningless leadership battles over who should lead in the next elections? The opposition party executives are no longer in front of the television cameras or the tape recorders. Are they appearing non-existent because elections are not around the corner? Some of their executive members were even competing for state contracts and hoping that they could be appointed into some government ministry or department.

So ordinary people ask, "Where are the opposition members when things are obviously going bad for the masses?" What they should be asking is whether the opposition politicians themselves understand their role in the society. It is the responsibility of political parties to educate the masses on questions of public policy and aspects of state governance. They should be able to ensure that the politicians in power are held to their knees and kept accountable to the general welfare of the society. Opposition parties should always critic public policy in tune with public opinion and public interest. They should be actively engaged in the education of the people around their political philosophy and party programs. But do the opposition parties in Sierra Leone understand this? In fact, where are the opposition parties in the first place? Without an organized opposition, democracy is nothing but a farce. When state actors develop the feeling that they can carry out their desires without resistance, the masses and the national resources are definitely at the mercy of politicians in power. Under such a situation, democracy faces a crisis and civil liberties are at risk.

This is why Ernest Koroma's style of governance must be checked continuously. The risk of relapsing into a passive one-party state in the country if the current trend of affairs is allowed to continue without resistance is imminent. Tendencies of authoritarian democracy are developing with the way Koroma is conducting the political affairs of the country. National institutions are compromised and can no longer function appropriately. The president's political appointments and decisions have hindered the independence of state institutions. Of tremendous concern today is the law enforcement agencies – the police and the judiciary – whose personnel act to satisfy the president and his party. Koroma has personalized governance and is quickly entrenching structures of state repression and coercion.

Police Officers and the Law

Very recently, the Sierra Leone Police announced that it was building a new police divisional headquarters in the outskirts of Makeni, the hometown of President Koroma. The construction project, estimated to worth around 500 million Leones, was launched by the president himself. Newspaper reports in Freetown said Ernest Koroma described the construction project as "indicative of development taking place in the country." "We need to provide the police with the necessary assistance to enable them respond adequately to the needs of the people of this country," Koroma reportedly said during the occasion. When completed, the new police station was expected to comprise ten offices, a conference hall, a modern secretariat and four detention facilities. Senior police officers in Freetown said the police station should be complete by the end of 2013. It will be the first police station in the country with facilities for disabled persons.

The launch of the new police station project by Koroma in Makeni coincided with the arrest and detention of opposition politician, Charles Francis Margai in Freetown by the Criminal Investigation Department (CID) of the Sierra Leone on allegations of "subversion." A pro-ruling party newspaper published photographs of a supposedly excited President Koroma during the launch of the project. APC propagandists reported that the President was satisfied with the police for "maintaining law and order across the country."

While this development was happening, questions were raised regarding police handling of cases dealing with opposition politicians and their supporters. Some opposition politicians suspected that the president's continued build-up of a "highly armed strong police force" represents an intention to create the equivalent of a police state in the country. Ruling party propagandists said they had to deal with "lawlessness" in the country. An assistant to the president even referred to opposition politicians and their supporters as "lawless individuals." Koroma himself was reported to have said in Makeni that: "prosperity does not exist in a society that is full of reckless talks and lawlessness."

Those watching ongoing police activities in the country during the recent period have not been highly impressed with the nature and style of policing conducted by officers of the police force. Opposition politicians in particular have been highly critical of police response to incidents involving opposition members and supporters across the country. They accused the police of brutality against defenseless citizens. Ordinary citizens have also randomly complained that police officers offer selective treatment in favor of those with political connection and material influence. They said the police only protect the politicians in power and those with finance to buy justice.

These complaints of biases by the police against opposition members and the ordinary citizens have persisted regardless of huge budgets allocated to the police department by government from tax-payers monies to standardize the professionalism of the country's police service. Police responses to citizens' protest against acts of injustice and inequality over the last few years did not only betray the level of bias, but it continually exposed the lack of police adherence to basic standards of acceptable policing methods. In the investigations of the police response to the mine workers protest against African Minerals in April 2012, the Human Rights Commission of Sierra Leone condemned the excessive use of force by the police to put down the protests. The Commission stated that the police violated the human rights of the workers and residents of the community. Similar incidents were also reported in Wellington and Goderich communities in Freetown. All incidents exemplified the level of police brutality and violence against innocent citizens in the country in recent times.

Capacity building of the police service should not be focused on building more police stations across the country. Neither should it be aimed at arming police officers with assault rifles and other sophisticated anti-riot equipment. Government finance to the police force should emphasize training and teaching programs for police officers to understand and appreciate the standards of acceptable policing methods. A police force that assumes an antagonistic position against the ordinary citizens of a country betrays its supposed duty to protect against injustice and repression, will surely find its task extremely difficult to discharge. To maintain stability and order in any country, the police force must be able to operate neutrally, independently and fairly. Modern-day policing methods requires officers to take into consideration the protection of ordinary citizens from repression and human rights abuse, regardless of whether they are opposition supporters or members. The police would have a task that is difficult to accomplish because it is largely and continually accused of being an instrument that is systematically used by ruling party officials to harass and intimate opposition leaders and their supporters.

Police officers should be conversant with the rules that govern human dignity and natural justice in carrying out their duties. It will be useless to spend hundreds of millions of tax-payers monies in building police stations and offices for police officers who are largely believed to be ignorant of standard instruments of modern policing methods. Spending huge budgets to build the infrastructural capacity of a police force, some of whose personnel had barely gone beyond high school, does not fully address the question of efficiency in the police service. The human resource capacity of the police force has to be built with the objective of creating a force of officers whose absolute loyalty should be with the people and the prescriptions of the law. Police officers should be free from the accusations and beliefs that their loyalty is only with officials of the party that comes to power at any given time.

This is why Ernest Koroma, the president, should have concentrated his efforts into realistically addressing the educational challenges confronting the country today. Creating additional infrastructural facilities for police officers is not the actual solution to crime and violence. The establishment of additional classrooms and better learning facilities for schools and colleges is what the country needs more than anything else. The money that is currently being used to build a new police divisional headquarters in Makeni, where there are already two existing police stations, is a misdirection of tax-payers funds. Those resources could have been utilized to build additional lecture halls at Fourah Bay College, for instance, where overcrowding makes it impossible for students and lecturers to properly attend classes.

Recently, the Vice Chancellor of Njala University, Prof. Abu Sesay, complained that the University was in need of funds to respond to the challenges of infrastructure. Other institutions across the country suffer from the same difficulty. So when government spends more money to build additional police stations in places like Makeni when schools and colleges across the country are starved of classroom facilities, it raises serious questions on the motives of such development undertakings.

There is a serious need to address the problems of our human resource development in the country. This requires a serious examination of the educational structures and institutions. The problems of crime and violence across the country today cannot be wholly addressed by building jails and police stations in every village and town. Neither is law and order going to be fully maintained through the deployment of armed police officers with assault rifles across every community in Sierra Leone. In fact, a recent survey by a local human rights group stated that crime rates have increased regardless of the presence of armed Operational Support Division (OSD) officers in various communities.

A highly literate and highly trained police force could better function with certain restraints. It is not a secret that many police recruits in recent times were drawn from the population of high school leavers and drop-outs. Some people even allege that recent police recruitments have specifically relied on the many unemployed ghetto youths across the country. Some of these youth had either been briefly detained in police cells for small-scale offences or had been involved in some aspect of political violence in the past. What will become of these youth when they are recruited into the police force?

Police officers and the youth they are policing require serious education and training in the first place. Ernest Koroma should have taken pride in building the infrastructural capacity of the country's educational institutions than the construction of new police stations and jails for officers whose level of education also requires development. A police force without an understanding of the rule of law is nothing but a group of men empowered to use the law against those for whom the law is supposed to protect.

This situation was clearly demonstrated in the police arrest and detention of opposition politician and leader of the Peoples Movement for Democratic Change (PMDC), Charles Francis Margai in May 2013. An examination of the events that preceded the arrest and the overall conduct of officers of the police force in dealing with the situation raised a number of questions. Foremost among these were the issues of law, constitutionality and equal treatment of all citizens by institutions of the state.

Margai was held on the night of May 10, 2013, for statements he allegedly made at a press conference in his Chambers a week earlier. During the said press conference, Margai expressed frustration over the failure of President Koroma to amicably settle a land dispute between himself and the first lady, Sia Nyama Koroma. Margai had alleged that the president was allowing his wife to use the service of the Sierra Leone police to deny him possession of his property, a piece of land situated at Cape Road in Aberdeen. He reported that personnel of the Operational Support Division (OSD), who were acting under the instructions of the president's wife, had gone to the said land and brutalized the caretaker and beaten-up his driver.

Margai squarely blamed the president for this act of intimidation and lawlessness because, according to him, Koroma failed to intervene despite a letter and personal visit he made to the president in relation to the issue. Police believed that Margai's statement bordered on a security concern. He was held on Friday night for what the police say constituted an act of "subversion." In particular, the police singled out the only sentence allegedly made by Margai: that he has 20,000 Kamajors, a civil defense force in the 1990s, at his command to defend him and his property should the need arise. That was the only sentence the police held on to build their case for arresting Margai.

This development engineered a huge debate across the country and beyond. As usual, the APC propagandists were the first to comment on the issue. They argued that Margai was arrested because of security concerns from the public. A pro-APC newspaper claimed that a particular youth group felt threatened by the utterances of Margai and called on the police to arrest him. Some members of the Sierra Leone Peoples Party (SLPP), on the other hand, say Margai built the monster that consumed him. In fact, an article on the *Unity Newspaper* of Monday May 13, 2013 stated that the APC showed Margai its true color. Ordinary people themselves were not left out on the debate. They also argued variedly on the issue.

But one fundamental aspect was left out in the whole debate: the circumstances that generated the supposedly vexed statement by Charles Margai for which he was arrested. What were the events that preceded the arrest? Or the circumstances that generated the pronouncement of the sentence that was singled out by the police? Were the police in violation of due process when they carried out the arrest of Margai? And what were the general implications of Margai's arrest and detention on the assumed democratic credentials of President Koroma?

The answers to these questions will help us to not only situate the contradiction into its proper perspective, but it will allow us to offer an understanding of the fundamental problems surrounding the nature of democracy and governance culture in the country. Charles Margai's arrest and detention offered the country an opportunity to examine the level of independence of the national democratic institutions. Are these institutions particularly functioning to protect the fundamental rights of citizens in accordance with the principles of the rule of law? Or are they being systematically used by ruling party officials to harass and intimidate opposition politicians and supporters? The controversy surrounding Charles Margai borders on a question of national democratic rights and individual liberties. It has little to do with the so-called national security that was talked about by the police and APC propagandists.

Charles Margai's arrest put into question the citizens' equal access to justice and their fair treatment and protection by the state. Far from the arguments by APC propagandists that Margai's arrest was in the interest of national security, the issue itself exposed the level of state repression and injustice against opposition politicians. Behind the venomous propaganda that emanated from the supposed "contentious statement" by Margai was the central question of selective treatment of citizens by the police.

It should not be forgotten that, before the said statement, Charles Margai had been very critical of the country's style of governance and its system of justice. He had expressed serious grievances relating to the violation of his constitutional rights by individuals connected to the presidency. He alleged in particular that the president's wife, Sia Nyama Koroma, used the police to perpetrate acts of intimidation and lawlessness calculated to deny him access to his property. Charles Margai had reportedly sought an amicable resolution to the problem by writing a letter to the president and also personally visiting him in respect to the allegation surrounding the first lady. When all these failed, Margai then revealed to the press that he intended to seek for a warrant of arrest against the president's wife for the alleged acts of trespass and other violations. Few hours later, Margai himself was arrested by the police on allegations of "subversion."

Minutes after the arrest, the police and ruling party propagandists immediately subsumed Charles Margai's grievances and complaints around the land issue, and substituted it with a discussion surrounding the supposed contentious sentence singled out by the police from Margai's statement. They argued that Margai had threatened the security of the country. Some even said he threatened the life of the president. Both the police and the APC propagandists were no longer willing to discuss the pertinent questions raised by Charles Margai. Neither were they keen on looking at the basis of the controversy that generated the statement for which Margai was arrested.

Many people doubted how the police and the APC propagandists could see Margai's statement a concern to national security, yet they could not find the alleged employment of police officers by the president's wife to intimidate and harass other Sierra Leoneans a serious violation of the country's constitution. It seemed the police were not even willing to talk about the supposed involvement of the president's wife and the police in the alleged discharge of acts of intimidation and brutality against defenseless citizens, which infuriated Margai in the first place. So Charles Margai's statement, whether it is considered subversive or otherwise, was the product of frustration that was caused by state repression and the excessive application of political authority. The supposed contentious statement by Margai could not have been made by him had the alleged conditions of brutality and violence, both physically and psychologically, not been present to begin with.

From this background, we have to question whether the police were just interested in protecting the politicians in power. Opposition politicians have regularly accused police officers of biases in favor of those in power. They often alleged that police protection is offered only to those with political and material influence or connections. When these accusations persist in a country, ordinary people lose faith and confidence in the national security institutions. And it gives way to thoughts of alternative self-defense as reportedly advanced by Charles Margai.

In any country where the ordinary citizens and opposition politicians in particular feel they are at the mercy of the state and those within the corridors of power, then the stability of that society is largely at risk. The question of the national security of any country is largely dependent upon the neutrality, independence, and fairness of the national institutions upholding its governance mechanism and structure. These national institutions include the police service, the judiciary and the other democratic institutions established to protect citizens from dictatorship and repression. They must act fairly and independently if the peace and stability of such a society is to be maintained.

This is the significance of Charles Margai's controversy. He forcefully ignited, through his arrest and detention, a public debate on the style of governance in the country, and by extension, placed the very democratic credentials of President Koroma to test. If nothing else, it questioned the independence of the country's judiciary and the neutrality of the police force in dealing with cases involving state actors and their immediate family members. Charles Margai's detention challenged Koroma's claim to democracy and was surely a dent on the assumed human rights credentials of the president. It exposed the country's seeming lack of adherence to the principles of the rule of law. These are the general implications. This is what Charles Margai sought to address with his protest. It was a direct confrontation against state repression and abuse of political power. Charles Margai's protest questioned the rule of law in the country.

Re-Positioning Democracy

It is therefore within this context that a fundamental question arises: how can the country overcome this anti-democratic situation? Answering this question requires a re-examination of the entire social system itself; it requires a social postmortem that goes at the heart of the society in a bid to diagnose the root causes of its many socio-political contradictions and economic challenges. This is a prerequisite.

A social investigation, conducted with a scientific approach towards society, will reveal the varied typologies of contradictions that exist among the masses and how they can be overturned. It is through such a process that questions of class stratification and resource exploitation, which are antagonisms resulting from policies and actions of the neocolonial state, can be unraveled. It is also by such method that the hypocrisy of the neocolonialist state and its idea of democracy can be fully exposed and eventually defeated.

This is what will re-position democracy and restore constitutionalism in a country. But democracy and constitutionalism cannot win in any country without a social transformation that destroys the class structure of the existing political order responsible for the current problems experienced in that society. To accomplish this, a scientific study of the society must be undertaken. The result of such an investigation must be a theory that answers the many questions raised or discovered by the investigation. It is such a theory that will produce both the organization and the program that challenge the order of authoritarian democracy. It is by this method and approach that Africans can prevent the continuous rise of despotic presidents and the ongoing triumph of the system of economic exploitation and political corruption that a state governed by authoritarian democrats engenders.

ACKNOWLEDGEMENTS

The publication of this collection of essays and articles into a book volume has been made possible with the diverse support of several family members and comrades. It is with pleasure that I acknowledge the various efforts and contributions of the following individuals whose inputs made this project a reality: Comrade Natalio Sowande Wheatley of the British Virgin Islands; Comrade Tommy Joshua in Philadelphia; Comrade Madieu Jalloh, Pios Foray in Freetown. I also appreciate Brother Cheik Amma Diop whose earlier comments, suggestions and inputs were absolutely tremendous.

A special recognition and appreciation is hereby given to the ongoing unconditional support rendered to my many projects by Comrade Matthew Willis. Thanks to my dear mother, Madam Lirwan Bah; and my sisters, Mariama and Lamrana for the continued encouragement and love. I also extend a special thank you to Mottie D. Innis of Maryland for the support and encouragement. My final words of appreciation go to Joshua McDermott and Jessica McDermott for their usual support to my work and family.

BIBLIOGRAPHY

Abdullah, Ibrahim: "Africans Do Not Live by Bread Alone: Against Greed, Not Grievance," *Africa Review of Books*, Vol.2 No.1 March, 2006 (pp 12-13).

Biney, Ama: *The Intellectual and Political Legacies of Kwame Nkrumah, Journal of Pan-African Studies*, vo14, no10, January 2012

Cabral, Amilcar: *The Weapon of Theory*, Havana, Cuba, January, 1966

Cesaire, Aime: "Discourse on Colonialism," *Monthly Review Press*, New York (2001)

Dukulé, Abdoulaye: "Guinea: The Next West African Crisis," *The Perspective*, Atlanta, 2005

Els, Frik: "How Former Guinean Dictator Lansana Conte Sold Guinea's $50 Billion Wealth for $0," *Africa Sun Times Online*, June 23, 2013

Fanon, Franz: *The Wretched of the Earth*

Furedi, Frank: *Colonial Wars and the Politics of Third World Nationalism*, London, 1994

Gassama, Ibrahim: "Africa and the Politics of Destruction: A Critical Re-Examination of Neocolonialism and Its Consequences", *Oregon Review of International Law*, Vol 10, No 2, 2008.

Guinea: Mining Laws and Regulations Handbook, Vol. 1, International Business Publications, USA 2012

Korten, David C: *When Corporations Rule the World*, Berrett-Koehler Publishers; 2nd edition (2001)

Momoh, Joseph: *Acceptance Speech: At the All People's Congress (A.P.C.)*, 9th National Delegates' Conference, Bintumani Conference Centre, Aberdeen, Freetown, 1st to 4th August, 1985

Nkrumah, Kwame: Neocolonialism, *The Last Stage of Imperialism*, Panaf, 1965
_ Class Struggle in Africa, Panaf, 2005
_ Africa Must Unite, International Publishers, 1970

Rodney, Walter: *How Europe Underdeveloped Africa*, Bogle-L'Ouverture, 1973

Sankoh, Mohamed: "A Joke Called the African Socialist Movement," *Torchlight newspaper*, 25 November 2009 pp3

The Rising Sun: A History of the All People's Congress Party of Sierra Leone, APC, 1982

Toure, Ahmed Sekou: *Africa on the Move*, Panaf, 2010

Weiss, Holger: *Framing a Radical African Atlantic: African American Agency, West African Intellectuals, and the International Trade Union Committee of Negro Workers*, Brill Academic Pub (December 31, 2013)

Wyse, Akintola J.G: *H. C. Bankole-Bright and Politics in Colonial Sierra Leone, 1919-1958*, Cambridge University Press, 1990

Zeilig, Leo: *Class Struggle and Resistance in Africa*, Haymarket Books (2009)

INDEX

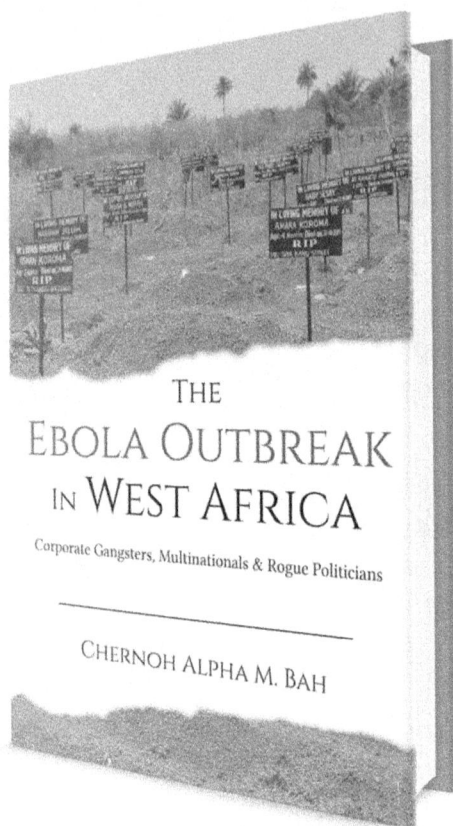

THE
EBOLA OUTBREAK
IN WEST AFRICA
Corporate Gangsters, Multinationals & Rogue Politicians

CHERNOH ALPHA M. BAH

Also available from the Africanist Press:

The Ebola Outbreak in West Africa:
Corporate Gangsters, Multinationals & Rogue Politicians

ISBN: 978-099-697392-2 (paperback)
978-099-697391-5 (Hardcover)

Publisher: Africanist Press
Author: Bah, Chernoh Alpha M.

Africanist Press books can be ordered through booksellers or by contacting
Africanist Press
Sales & Distribution Department
738 Washington Avenue (Apt 1A)
Brooklyn, NY 11238
+1 (347) 569-1978
africanistpress100@gmail.com

www.ingramcontent.com/pod-product-compliance
Lightning Source LLC
Chambersburg PA
CBHW020258030426
42336CB00010B/824